FINANCIAL TURNAROUND
STRATEGY OF
SAURASHTRA UNIVERSITY

:: Author ::

Hetal Shah
(M.com., NET.,M.Phil)

PUBLISHED BY

The New Era International Publishing House
HQ. At & Po. Chaveli., Ta- Chansma,
Dist- Patan, North Gujarat, India, Asia.
www.iphouseindia.com

First Publication: 1ST JULY, 2015

ISBN:- 978-1-51486-605-4

Price: Rs.800/- INDIA

$ 15 OUTSIDE INDIA

PUBLISHED BY

**The New Era International Publishing House
HQ. At & Po. Chaveli., Ta- Chansma,
Dist- Patan, North Gujarat, India, Asia.
www.iphouseindia.com**

PREFACE

It is a pleasure to present this book before our learned readers. It will give basic idea to readers regarding management theory, turnaround strategy, history and growth of university, and different techniques of accounting for analyze, and interpretation of financial statements. The author has presented the whole framework of research methodology chapter which will be an aid for future researchers. It covers explanation of different terminologies used in university financial statements for preparation and presentation.

In this book author has applied common size technique for analyzing the data. Ratios related with university accounts are framed by the author for the research work. In the end of the book observations and suggestion of author are sited.

This book will became a literature review for the future researchers who want to do research on universities.

Author hopes that the students, researchers, practitioners and end-users would find the reading of this book highly interesting and useful. She feels that her efforts are amply rewarded if the book serves the purpose for which it is prepared. Suggestion for the improvement of the book from every corner is most appreciable.

HETAL SHAH

BHUJ-KACHCHH

INDEX

Chapter	TITLE	Page No.
	List of Tables	
	List of Graphs	
1.	**CONCEPTUAL INTRODUCTION**	**1-25**
	1.1 Importance of Management	1
	1.2 Meaning of Management	2
	1.3 Process of Management	3
	1.4 Difference between Management & Leadership	4
	1.5 Principles of Management	5
	1.6 Management Standards	8
	1.7 Genesis of Strategic Management	11
	a) What is strategy?	11
	b) Developing of Strategy	12
	c) Role of Strategic Management	13
	d) Type of Strategy	15
	e) Turnaround Strategy	20
2.	**RESEARCH DESIGN**	**26-41**
	2.1 Research Problem	26
	2.2 Objectives of the Research study	28

2.3 Hypothesis of the Research study   28

2.4 Research Methodology / Tools   29

     1. Data collection   29

     2. Methods of Research   29

2.5 Period of the Research Study   36

2.6 Limitations of the Research study   36

2.7 Review of Literature   38

3. UNIVERSITY DEVELOPMENT IN INDIA   **42-63**

3.1 Genesis and Early History   42

3.2 Concept of University   45

     a) First Test   45

     b) Second Test   45

3.3 The Modern Meaning of the word University   46

3.4 Earlier Systems and Institutions – A Comparison   47

3.5 The First Universities   48

3.6 Universities in Post Independence Period   53

3.7 Specialized Universities   54

3.8 Specialized Institutions of Higher Learning   56

a) Institutions recognized as "Deemed Universities"   56

	b) Institutions of National Importance	58
	3.9 Open University	59
	3.10 Introduction of Study Unit – Saurashtra University	61
4.	**ANALYSIS OF DATA**	**64-165**
	4.1 Meaning of Not For Profit Organizations	64
	4.2 Fund Based Accounting	65
	4.3 Explanation of Revenue and Capital Sources of Income and Expenditure of Saurashtra University	68
	4.4 Analysis of Revenue Income Aspect by common size method	80
	4.5 Analysis of Revenue Expenditure Aspect by Common Size Method	93
	4.6 Ratio Analysis	110
5.	**FINDINGS AND CONCLUSIONS**	**166-174**
	5.1 Findings	166
	5.2 Conclusions	174
	Bibliography	**177-179**

LIST OF TABLES

Table No.	Heading of Table	Page No.
3.1	Universities Established in the Pre-Independence Period	51
3.2	List of some of the Institutions recognized as 'Deemed Universities' after Independence	57
3.3	List of Institutions of National Importance	58
4.0	Revenue Fund Income Sources in Common size form	79
4.1	Table explaining criteria for type of share in total revenue income expenditure	80
4.2	Revenue Fund Expenditure Sources in Common size form	93
4.3	Post Graduate Department Expenditure to Income Ratio	111
4.4	Ttest calculation and Ttest result of Post Graduate Department Expenditure to Income ratio and Correlation Co-efficient of ratio	114
4.5	Examination Expenditure to Income Ratio	116
4.6	Ttest calculation and Ttest result of examination ratio and Correlation Co-	120

efficient

4.7	Library Expenditure to Income Ratio	122
4.8	Ttest calculation and Ttest result of Library ratio and Correlation Co-efficient	125
4.9	Hostel Expenditure to Income Ratio	127
4.10	Ttest calculation and Ttest result of hostel ratio and Correlation Co-efficient	130
4.11	Estate Expenditure to Income Ratio	132
4.12	Ttest calculation and Ttest result of Estate ratio and Correlation Co-efficient	135
4.13	Salary Expenditure of University Employees to State Government Maintenance Grant Ratio	138
4.14	Ttest calculation and Ttest result of ratio and Correlation Co-efficient	141
4.15	Administrative Expenditure to State Government Maintenance Grant Ratio	144
4.16	Ttest calculation and Ttest result of ratio and Correlation Co-efficient	147
4.17	Total of salary expenditure, administrative expenditure and deficit/surplus of Post Graduate Department, Library, Hostel, Estate	150

4.18   Total of salary expenditure, administrative expenditure and deficit/surplus of Post Graduate Department, Library, Hostel, Estate to State Government Maintenance Grant Ratio   151

4.19   Health Centre Expenditure to Other Fees Income Ratio   154

4.20   Net Surplus or Deficit transferred to General Fund A/C including exam fees and excluding exam fees   156

LIST OF CHARTS

Chart No.	Heading of Chart	Page No.
4a	Tuitions and Other Fees of Post Graduate Share in Total Revenue Income	82
4b	Exam Fees Share in Total Revenue Income	84
4c	Other Fees Share in Total Revenue Income	88
4d	State Government Maintenance Grant Share in Total Revenue Income	91
4e	Post Graduate Education & Research Share in Total Revenue Expenditure	95
4f	Examination Expense Share in Total Revenue Expenditure	96

4g	Salary Expenditure of university employees Share in Total Revenue Expenditure	102
4h	Administrative Expenditure Share in Total Revenue Expenditure	104
4i	Post Graduate Department Expenditure to Income Ratio	113
4j	Examination Department Expenditure to Income Ratio	117
4k	Examination Department Net Surplus Yearly	119
4l	Library Expenditure to Income Ratio	124
4m	Hostel Expenditure to Income Ratio	129
4n	Estate Expenditure to Income Ratio	134
4o	Salary Expenditure to State Government Maintenance Grant Ratio and State Government Grant Net	140
4p	Administrative Expenditure to State Government Maintenance Grant Ratio	146
4q	Net Deficit or Surplus of State Government Grant after meeting all main expenditure	153

CHAPTER: 1
CONCEPTUAL INTRODUCTION

1.1 IMPORTANCE OF MANAGEMENT

Management is a universally necessary function. It is essential for all kinds of organizations, whether they be business organizations or non-business organizations. This is so because every organization requires the making of decisions, the coordinating of activities, the handling of people, and evaluating the performance directed towards its objectives. This task for the organization is performed by that responsible person called the Manager. He brings the principal resource – human talent into combination with non-human resources, viz., machines, materials and money. Every organization, therefore have managers or the heads who has to play the role for the management of finance, resources and human resource together. The managers or the heads may be called supervisors, directors, superintendents, agency chiefs, or foreman but managers are present. In other words, management takes place at all levels in the organizational hierarchy. Every manager performs essentially the same functions whether he belongs to the top or middle or first-line management. The only difference is in the magnitude of the task and the scope and degree of the authority. Qualified managers, therefore, are important both to their firms and to the future of society. They are so important that high quality management is a **firm's single most important resource.**

1.2 MEANING OF MANAGEMENT

In general usage, the word management identifies a special group of people who direct effort towards common objectives through the activities of other people. Simply stated management "gets things done through other people". This makes the important point that it is a purposeful activity. It could be extended to read: 'Management is about deciding what to do and then getting it done through the people.' But there is some more, correctly the definition emphasizes that people are the most important resources available to the managers. It is through this resource that other resources are managed. However, managers are ultimately accountable for the management of all other resources, including their own. The definition of management should therefore be amended to: 'Deciding what to do and then getting it done through the effective use of resources'.

1.3 THE PROCESS OF MANAGEMENT

The overall process of management is divided into a number of individual processes which are methods of operation specially designed to assist in the achievement of objectives. Their purpose is to bring as much system, order, predictability, logic and consistency to the task of management as possible in the ever changing, varied and turbulent environment in which managers works.

The main process of management was defined by the classical theorists of management such as Henri Fayol as:

a. **Planning** – deciding on a course of action to achieve a desired result;

b. **Organizing** – setting up and staffing the most appropriate organization to achieve the aim;

c. **Motivating** – exercising leadership to motivate people to work together smoothly and to the best of their ability as part of a team;

d. **Controlling** – measuring and monitoring the progress of work in relation to the plan and taking corrective action when required.

1.4 DIFFERENCE BETWEEN MANAGEMENT AND LEADERSHIP

MANAGEMENT is concerned with achieving results by effectively obtaining deploying, utilizing and controlling all the resources required, namely people, money, facilities, plant and equipment, information and knowledge.

LEADERSHIP focuses on the most important resource, people. It is the process of developing and communicating a vision for the future, motivating people and gaining their commitment and engagement.

1.5 PRINCIPLES OF MANAGEMENT

A principle means a fundamental truth on the basis of reasoning, a primary element of general law. Principles of management do not take principal of physical sciences. They are such guidelines which come to the help of managers.

Henry Fayol gave the following fourteen principles of management –

a) Division of Work :

The work is divided in such a way that it promotes specialization and one person does only one thing rather than doing every thing himself.

b) Parity between Authority and Responsibility :

Authority and responsibility go side by side and should be commensurate to each other.

c) Discipline :

Discipline is in essence obedience, application, energy behavior and outward marks of respect observed in accordance with the standing agreements between the firm and its employees.

d) Unity of Command :

One person should receive order from one superior only.

e) Unity of Direction :

There should be one head and one plan for a group of activities having the same objectives.

f) Subordination of Individual Interest to General Interest :

Fayol was of the opinion that the interest of one employee or a group of employees should not prevail the interest of the enterprise as a whole. Management should make efforts to reconcile individual interests with common interests.

g) Fair Remuneration to Workers :

Fayol wanted the remuneration to be paid to employees should be fair and should afford maximum satisfaction to both employees and the employer.

h) Effective Centralization :

Fayol favored centralization of powers with the top management.

i) Scalar Chain :

Fayol was of the opinion that a hierarchic channel called the scalar chain is necessary to ensure unity of command and effective communication. However, a gang plank may be created by establishing a line of authority, to facilitate quick communication. However, a gang plank may be created by passing the established line of authority, to facilitate quick communication.

j) Order :

It means the right man in the right job and right material in the right place. Material order means a proper place for everything and everything in its right place.

k) Equity :

It means justice and kindness. Fayol was of the opinion that to encourage workers to fulfill their duties with devotion and loyalty, management should deal with the workers with equity – based on Kindness and justice.

l) Stability in Tenure :

Fayol felt that instability of personnel is both the cause and effect of bad management so there should be stability in tenure.

m) Initiative :

Employees should be given the chance and opportunity in taking initiative in deciding and implementing the plans.

n) Esprit de corps :

It refers to harmony and mutual understanding among the member of the organization.

1.6 MANAGEMENT STANDARDS

Management standards define what professional managers need to know and be able to do. They therefore serve as guides on what is expected of managers, as checklists against which performance can be assessed, and as the basis for management qualifications. The following management standards have been produced by the Management Standards Centre:

a) PROVIDING DIRECTION

- develop a vision for the future;
- gain commitment and provide leadership;
- provide governance – comply with values, ethical and legal frameworks and manage risks in line with shared goals;

b) FACILITATE CHANGE

- lead innovations;
- manage change;

c) ACHIEVING RESULTS

- lead the business to achieve goals and objectives;
- lead operations to achieve specific results;
- lead projects to achieve specified results;

d) MEETING CUSTOMER NEEDS

- promote products and/or services to customers;

- obtain contracts to supply products and/ or services;

- deliver products and/or services to customers;

- solve problems for customers;

e) WORKING WITH PEOPLE

- build relationships;

- develop networks and partnerships;

- manage people

f) USING RESOURCES

- manage financial resources;

- procure products and/or services;

- manage physical resources and technology;

- manage information and knowledge;

g) MANAGING SELF AND PERSONAL SKILLS

- manage own contribution;

- develop own knowledge, skills and competence;

1.7 GENESIS OF STRATEGIC MANAGEMENT

In genesis of strategic management let us understand the following heads:-

a) WHAT IS STRATEGY?

Strategy consists of a statement or an understanding of what the organization or a part of it wants to become, where it wants to go and broadly, how it means to get there. Business strategy in a commercial enterprise answers the questions: 'What business are we in?' and 'How are we going to make money out of it?' Strategy determines the direction in which the enterprise is going in relation to its environment in order to achieve sustainable competitive advantage. The emphasis is on focused actions that differentiate the firm from its competitors. It is a declaration of intent which defines means to achieve ends, and is concerned with the long-term allocation of significant resources and with the long-term allocation of significant resources and with matching those resources and capabilities to the external environment. Strategy is a perspective on the way in which critical issues or success factors can be addressed, and strategic decisions aim to make a major and long-term impact on the behavior and success of the organization.

Individual managers develop strategies for the accomplishment of their longer-term objectives. Again these are directions of intent and definitions of how it is proposed those intentions should be put into effect.

Strategies are developed to provide for the realization of visions – views on when the future should be. Shared vision can be inspirational.

b) DEVELOPING STRATEGY

The formulation of strategy can be defined as a process for developing a sense of direction. It has often been described as a logical, step-by-step affair, the outcome of which is a formal written statement which provides a definitive guide to the organization's or the manager's long-term intentions. Many people still believe and act as if this was the case, but it is a misrepresentation of reality. This is not to dismiss completely the ideal of adopting a systematic approach – it has its uses as a means of providing an analytical framework for strategic decision making and a reference point for monitoring the implementation of strategy. But in practice the formulation of strategy can never be as rational and linear process as some managers attempt to make it.

c) THE ROLE OF STRATEGIC MANAGEMENT

Strategic management means that managers are looking ahead at what they need to achieve in the middle or relatively distant future. Although, they are aware of the fact that businesses, like managers, must perform well in the present to succeed in the future, they are concerned with the broader issues they are facing and the general directions in which they must go to deal with these issues and achieve longer-term objectives. They do not take a narrow or restricted view.

The purpose of strategic management is mainly to 'elicit the present actions for the future' and become 'action vehicles – integrating and institutionalizing mechanisms for change'. There is one saying 'Strong leaders articulate direction and save the organization from change by drift... They see a vision of the future that allows them to see more clearly what steps to take, building on present capacities and strengths.'

Strategic management deals with both ends and means. As an end it describes a vision of what something will look like in a few years' time. As a means, it shows how it is expected that the vision will be realized. Strategic management is therefore visionary management, concerned with creating and conceptualizing ideas of where the organization should be going. But it is also empirical management which decides how in practice it is going to get there.

The focus is on identifying the organization's mission and strategies, but attention is also given to the resource base required. It is necessary to remember that strategy is the means to create value. Managers who think strategically will have a broad and long-term view where they are going. They will also be aware that they are responsible, first, for planning how to allocate resources to opportunities which contribute to the implementation of strategy, second, for managing these opportunities in ways which will significantly add value to the results achieved by the firm, and third, for refining the strategy to meet new demands.

d) TYPE OF STRATEGIES

There are mainly two types of strategies:-

1. Generic Strategies
2. Grand Strategies

1. GENERIC STRATEGIES

Many planning experts believe that the general philosophy of doing business declared by the firm in the mission statement must be translated into a holistic statement of the firm's strategic orientation before it can further defined in terms of a specific long-term strategy. In other words, a long term or grand strategy must be based on a core idea about how the firm can best compete in the marketplace.

The popular term for this core idea is Generic Strategy. From a scheme developed by Michael Portor, many planners believe that any long-term strategy should derive from a firm's attempt to seek a competitive advantage based on one of three generic strategies:

i. Striving for overall low-cost leadership in the industry.

ii. Striving to create and market unique products for varied customer groups through differentiation.

iii. Striving to have special appeal to one or more groups of consumer or industrial buyers, focusing on their cost or differentiation concerns.

Advocates of generic strategies believe that each of these options can produce above-average returns for a firm in an industry. However, they are successful for very different reasons.

The product attribute also can be the marketing channels through which it is delivered, its image for excellence, the features it includes, and the service network that supports it. As a result of the importance of these attributes, competitors often face "Perceptual" barriers to entry when customers of a successfully differentiated firm fail to see largely identical products as being interchangeable. For example, General Motors hopes that customers will accept "only genuine GM replacement parts".

A focus strategy, whether anchored in a low-cost base or a differentiation base, attempts to attend to the needs of a particular market segment. Likely segments are those that are ignored by marketing appeals to easily accessible markets, to the "typical" customer or to customers with common applications for the product. Brick producers that typically service a radius of less than 100 miles and commuter airlines that serve regional geographic areas are other examples of industries where a focus strategy frequently yields above-average industry profits.

While each of the generic strategies enables a firm to maximize certain competitive advantages, each one also exposes the firm to a number of competitive risks. For example, a low-cost leader fears a new low-cost technology that is being developed by a competitor; a differentiating firm fears imitators; and a focused firm fears invasion by a firm that largely targets customers. As exhibit each generic strategy presents the firm with a number of risks.

2. GRAND STRATEGIES

While the need for firms to develop generic strategies remains an unresolved debate, designers of planning systems agree about the critical role of grand strategies. Grand strategies, often called master or business strategies provide basic direction for strategic actions. They are the basis of coordinated and sustained efforts directed toward achieving long-term business objectives.

Grand strategies indicate time period over which long-range objectives are to be achieved. Thus, a grand strategy can be defined as a comprehensive general approach that guides a firm's major actions.

The 15 principal grand strategies are:

I. Concentrated Growth

II. Market Development

III. Product Development

IV. Innovation

V. Horizontal Integration

VI. Vertical Integration

VII. Concentric Diversification

VIII. Conglomerate Diversification

IX. **Turn Around**

X. Divestiture

XI. Liquidation

XII. Bankruptcy

XIII. Joint Ventures

XIV. Strategic Alliances

XV. Consortia

Any one of these strategies could serve as the basis for achieving the major long-term objectives of a single firm. But a firm involved with multiple industries, business, product lines, or customers groups – as many firms are – usually combines several grand strategies.

e) TURN AROUND STRATEGY

For anyone of a large number of reasons, a firm can find itself with declining profits. Among these reasons are economic recessions, production inefficiencies, and innovative breakthroughs by competitors. In many cases, strategic managers believe that such a firm can survive and eventually recover if a concerted effort is made over a period of a few years to fortify its distinctive competences. This grand strategy is known as turn around. It typically is begun through one of two forms of retrenchment, employed singly or in combination:

Cost Reduction

Examples include decreasing the work force through employee attrition, leasing rather than purchasing equipment, extending the life of machinery, eliminating elaborate promotional activities, laying off employees, dropping items from a production line, and discontinuing low – margin customers.

Asset Reduction

Examples include the sale of land, buildings, and equipment not essential to the basic activity of the firm and the elimination of "perks," such as the company airplane and executives' cars.

Interestingly, the turnaround most commonly associated with this approach is in management positions. In a study of 58 large firms, researchers Shendel, Patton, and Riggs found that **turnaround almost always was associated with changes in top management.** Bringing in new managers was believed to introduce needed new perspectives on the firm's situation, to raise employee morale, and to facilitate drastic actions, such as deep budgetary cuts in established programs.

Strategic management research provides evidence that the firms that have used a turnaround strategy have successfully confronted decline. The research findings have been assimilated and used as the building blocks for a model of the turnaround process shown in 3.1

The model begins with a depiction of external and internal factors as causes of a firm's performance downturn. When these factors continue to detrimentally impact the firm, its financial health is threatened. Unchecked decline places the firm in a turnaround situation.

A turnaround situation represents absolute and relative-to-industry declining performance of a sufficient magnitude to explicit warrant turnaround actions. Turnaround situations may be the result of years of gradual slow down or months of sharp decline. In either case, the recovery phase of the turnaround process is likely to be more successful in accomplishing turnaround when it is preceded by planned retrenchment that result in the achievement of near-term financial stabilization. For a declining firm, stabilizing operations and restoring profitability almost always entail strict cost reduction followed by a shrinking back to those segments of the business that have the best prospects of attractive profit margins. The need for retrenchment was reflected in unemployment figures during the 2000-2003 recessions. More layoffs of American workers were announced in 2001 than in any of the previous eight years when U.S. companies announced nearly 2 million layoffs as the economy sunk into its first recession in a decade.

3.1 A model of the Turnaround Process

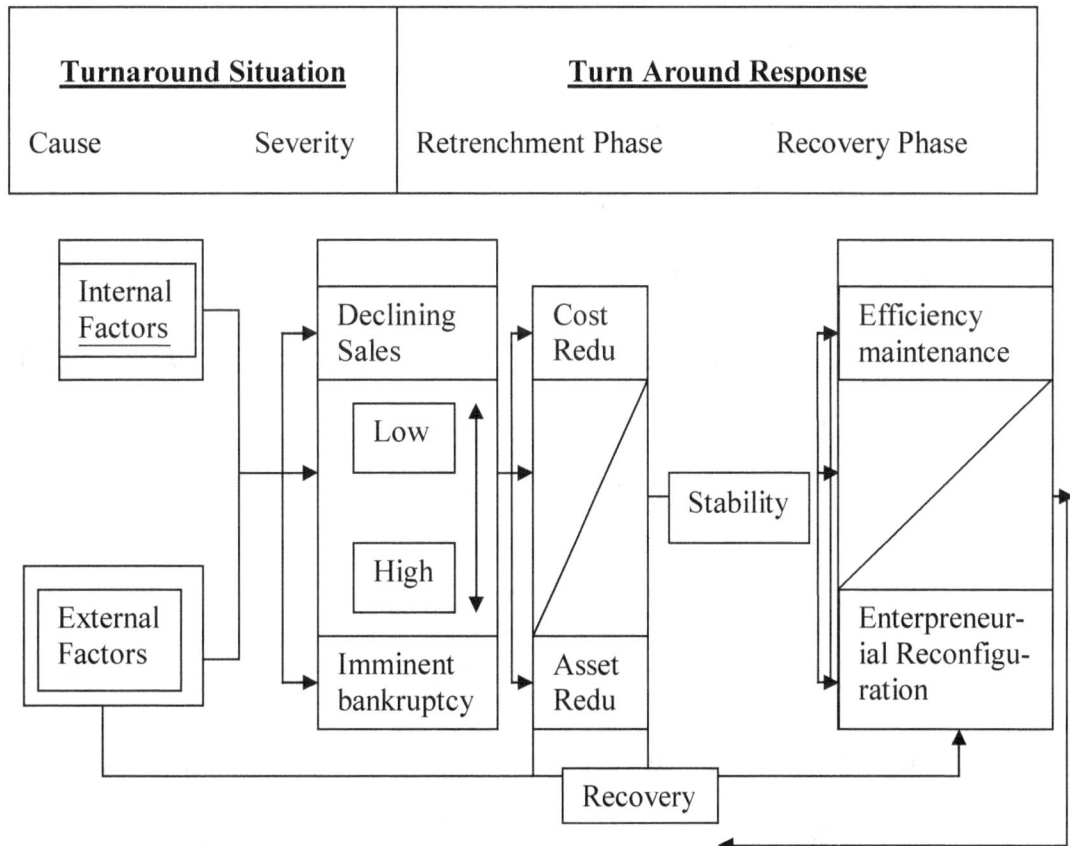

The immediacy of the resulting threat to company survival posed by the turnaround situation is known as situation severity. Severity is the governing factor in estimating the speed with which the retrenchment response will be formulated and activated. When severity is low, a firm has some financial cushion. Stability may be achieved through cost retrenchment alone. When turnaround situation severity is high, a firm must immediately stabilize the decline or bankruptcy is forthcoming. Cost reduction must be supplemented with more drastic asset reduction measures. Assets targeted for divestiture are those determined to be underproductive. In contrast, more productive resources are protected from cuts and represent critical elements of the future cost business plan of the company (that is the intended recovery response).

Turn around responses among successful firms typically include two stages of strategic activities – retrenchment and the recovery response. Retrenchment consists of cost-cutting and asset-reducing activities. The primary objective of the retrenchment phase is to stabilize the firm's financial condition. Situation severity has been associated with retrenchment responses among successful turnaround firms. Firms in danger of bankruptcy or failure attempt to halt decline through cost and asset reductions. Firms in less severe situations have achieved stability merely through cost retrenchment. However, in either case, for firms facing declining financial performance, the key to successful turnaround rests in the effective and efficient management of the retrenchment process.

The primary causes of the turnaround situation have been associated with the second phase of the turnaround process, the recovery response. For firms that declined primarily as a result of external problems, turnaround most often has been achieved through creative new entrepreneurial strategies. For firms that declined primarily as a result of internal problems, turnaround has been most frequently achieved through efficiency strategies. Recovery is achieved when economic measures indicate that the firm has regained its pre downturn levels of performance.

CHAPTER: 2
RESEARCH DESIGN

2.1 RESEARCH PROBLEM

"Globalization demands change in the existing structure, management and mode of delivery of education system. The challenge before universities is to provide the student's with the proper global competencies and well appropriate environment. The world economy is experiencing unprecedented changes. New developments in science and technology, media revolution and globalization are revolutionizing the education sector.

"In the context of a rapidly changing global economy, universities have to cope with the emerging challenges and becoming competitive. Private institutions are increasing; universities have to compete more and more with private sector institutions to generate additional resources because government is not in favor of being the sole financier of higher education. This will create necessity for universities to offer their disciplines more effectively and provide maximum satisfaction to their client group. Universities have to offer new educational disciplines and produce human resources who will meet the challenges of the emerging competitive economy.

"As we know that the universities are to respond to the challenges and uncertainties of new millennium, universities need the leaders who have strategic vision, well versed with latest techniques of management, financial management, capable of leading a team in addition to performing routine functions. In the present university environment traditional role of the administration is fast changing in view of the technological advancements resulting network culture with greater opportunities for growth, experimentation and innovations, professional development of administrators assumes new significance." (Jacket)

For all these activities university needs finance. And most of the universities facing the problem of financial crisis, and efficient management and this create the need to study their structure and analyze it. To solve this problem the sample Selection is **Saurashtra University** and the title of the dissertation is "Financial Turn Around Strategy of Saurashtra University".

2.2 OBJECTIVES OF THE RESEARCH STUDY

The major objectives with which this study has been carried out are as follows:-

1) To review the surplus/deficit position of Saurashtra university.

2) To analyze the main sources of revenues of Saurashtra university

3) To analyze the main sources of expenditure of Saurashtra university.

4) To make the suggestions for improvement of financial soundness and management in university.

2.3 HYPOTHESIS OF THE RESEARCH STUDY

1) Saurashtra University is facing the problem of financial deficit.

2) Revenue and Expenditure of all the departments of Saurashtra University are in equal proportion.

3) Deficit of Saurashtra University is due to inefficient financial management.

2.4 Research Methodology / Tools

1. Data collection

The collection of data refers to a purposive gathering of information relevant to the subject-matter of the study from the units under investigation. The collection of data can be of two types:-

- **Primary Data**
- **Secondary Data**

The data is of secondary type. The form of data is annual reports of Saurashtra University. The researcher has collected this data directly from Saurashtra University.

2 Methods of Research

Tools and Techniques of Analysis:

The following two types of tools and techniques of analysis have been used:

A) Accounting Techniques

B) Statistical Techniques

The researcher pick up the technique to suit their requirement and also on the basis of data available to them. The accounting techniques which are used for the analysis of financial statements of Saurashtra University are as follows:-

1. Common Size Statements

Common Size Statements is a useful way of analyzing financial statatements. Here, the financial statements are converted into common size statements by expressing absolute rupee amounts into percentages. When this method is pursued, the income statement exhibits each expense item or group of expense items as a percentage of net sales or here we have university as a percentage of total expense and total expense are taken as 100 percent. Similarly each income item or group of income items as a percentage of total income and total income are taken as 100 percent. Similarly each individual asset and liability classification is shown as a percentage of total assets and liabilities respectively. Statements preferred in this way are referred to as common size statements.

Common size statements prepared for one university over the years would highlight relative changes in each group of expenses, income, assets and liabilities.

2. Trend Analysis

Trend Analysis involve a comparison of the expenditure, income, assets and liabilities of a firm over a time, that is, present expenditure head is compared with the past expenditure head for the same firm. Similarly, with income, assets and liabilities also, Trend analysis indicates the direction of change in the expenditure, - improvement, deterioration or constancy over the years.

3. Ratio Analysis

Ratio may be based on figures in the balance sheet, Income and Expenditure A/c and both it is indicating profitability and efficiency of control over expenses are calculated on the basis of Income and Expenditure A/c. The Importance of accounting ratios is that it establishes relationship among various accounting data which are mutually interdependent and which influence each- other in a significant manner. This Ratio is also used to indicate the present position.

B) Statistical Techniques:

Use of statistical techniques has become a normal phenomenon in any type of analysis. Statistical analysis or tools which are used for financial analysis, Index numbers, regression analysis, Diagrammatic and graphic presentation of data has been made whenever necessary of the present study. The researcher picks up the techniques of "T" test for testing hypothesis relating to various variables of expenditure and income of university under study. The comparison of the variables becomes easy with statistical analysis.

Standard deviation is one of the best tool for the better result; It is defined as the square – root of the average of squares of deviations, when such deviations for the vales of individual items in a series are obtained from the arithmetic average. It is also less affected by fluctuations of sampling; SD is used in research studies and is regarded as a very satisfactory measure of dispersion in a series.

1. Arithmetic Mean

Measures of central tendency, known as statistical average mean, and arithmetic average it is the most common measure of central tendency and may be defined as the value which researcher get by dividing the total of the value of various items given in a series by the total numbers of items It is a relatively stable measure of central tendency. But it suffers from some limitations. However, mean is better than the other average.

2. "T" Test

'T' test if based on "T" distribution and it is considered an appropriate test for judging the significance of a sample mean or for judging the significance of difference between the means of two sample in case of small samples. When population variance is related or not, to know that we use paired 'T' test it can also be used for judging the significance of the co-efficient of simple and partial correlations. The relevant test statistic, 'T' test is calculated from the sample data and then compared with its probable value based on 'T' distribution for different levels of significance for different degrees of freedom at specific levels of significance for accepting or rejecting the null hypothesis. It may be noted the 'T' test applies only in case of small samples when population variance is unknown.

If a random sample x_1, x_2, ..., x_n of n values be drawn from a normal population with mean $\square$ and standard deviations then the mean of sample

$$\bar{x} = \frac{\Sigma x_i}{n}$$

Estimate of the variance: Let s^2 be the estimate of the variance of the sample then s^2 given by

$$s^2 = \frac{\Sigma(x_i - \bar{x})^2}{n-1}$$

(n - 1) as denominator in place 'n'.

(I) The statistic 't' is defined as

$$t = \frac{|\bar{x} - \mu|}{\sqrt{\frac{s^2}{n}}} \quad \text{or} \quad \frac{|\bar{x} - \mu|}{s}\sqrt{n}$$

Where x = sample mean, $\square$ = actual or hypothetical mean of population, n = sample size, s = standard deviation of sample.

Where s = $\sqrt{\dfrac{\Sigma\left(x_i - \bar{x}\right)^2}{n-1}}$

Note: 't' is distributed as the student distribution with (n - 1) degree of freedom (df).

3. Correlation Coefficient

Correlation is a statistical technique which measures and analyses the degree. The degrees are expressed by a coefficient ranges between -1 and + 1. It was defined by W.I.King as "Correlation means that between two series or groups of data there exist some casual connection."

The use of correlation is done in both - physical and social science but we shall confine our selves to the later and particularly to the field of business and commerce.

The value of ' t ' is calculated by finding out the ratio between the coefficient of correlation and its S. E.

$$t = \frac{r\sqrt{n-2}}{\sqrt{1-r^2}}$$

2.5 Period of the research study (1997 to 2005)

The study was under taken with reference to the period from 1996-1997 to 2004-2005. The period of research is of **nine years.**

2.6 Limitations of the Research Study

This study is based on the secondary data as well as supplementary data providing Financial Details only. It does not study the productivity aspects. It is also restricted to only one university – Saurashtra University. It also studies the period which in general also was of the Financial (fund) Crisis and that Govt.'s aptitude for the economic reforms in higher education was not that keen or encouraging. This will have its shadow impact on the Finance of Universities.

While carrying out the research, the researcher is fully aware of its following limitations:

1) As the work is based on the published data, the difference of purpose can marginally effect the conclusions drawn from it.

2) The validity of some of the data cannot be fully guaranteed particularly the cost data which are subject to some limitations.

3) Non-availability of the information as required by the researcher forms the major limitations of the study.

4) Saurashtra University is of Gujarat State University so it may happen that the financing of the study would not be relevant to other Universities.

5) Universities are not profit making organizations. But this study is based solely on the functioning of the business organizations and wants to give suggestions to improve financial health of the University.

6) As seen above, this study is related to nature and causes of financial deficit with respect to Saurashtra University which is related with Gujarat State.

Hence, this study will not be relevant to other parts of India.

2.7 Review of Literature

1. Performance Measurement in Non-Profit Organization – by James Cutt

It is generally accepted that a sufficient and appropriate definition of performance in non profit organization require multiple components. Such a multiple component definition is much more useful if it can serve not only retrospectively as a frame work for performance reporting but also prospectively and continuously as an information framework for both governance and management control over the cycle of organizational activities. By defining focus and causal integration the balance score card developed for commercial organization offers one useful way of transforming a multiple component performance reporting framework into a comprehensive governance and management information framework. The scorecard can be adapted for direct use in public sector commercial organizations with more creativity – involving the redefinition of focus as maximization off.

2. Methodological Problem to measure university efficiency in relation with its geographic localization
by, A. García-Aracil, D. Palomares-Montero

Institute for Innovation and Knowledge Management, INGENIO (CSIC-UPV Valencia/Spain)

This paper examines data on Spanish Public Universities for 2002 to 2004 to determine the geographical location of the most efficient universities, that is, we aim to identify whether the universities located in the richest regions are more efficient than those in the poorest regions. We employ Data Envelopment Analysis (DEA), a robust nonparametric frontier technique that enables us to benchmark and rank decision-making units. DEA applies multiple inputs and outputs to measure the efficiency of the universities. The results on whether there is a relation between university efficiency and the wealth of the region show that the richest regions have more higher education institutions, universities and that the universities located in rich regions are more efficient than those in poor regions

3. Dr. Maturs S.P. 2001

"Financial management in Indian Universities has studied the comparative structure of income and expenditure of B.H.U. Aligardh muslim University

4. Bray,M. (2000)

Financing Higher Education; Patterns, Trends and Options; Prospects 30, no.3:331-348.

5. Arumugam P (1999)

Roll of state and local bodies in financing education in Tamil Nadu, journal of education planning and administration

6. Bray,M. (1998)

Financing Education in developing Asia : Issues, Trends, and Policy Implications; Asian Development bank, manila.

7. Balachandra K K (1992)

Higher education in India: quest for and alternative financing system, University News.

8. Balachandra K K (1991)

Funding of state universities in India, some crucial issues journal of education, planning and administration

9. Agrawal R B (1992)

Financing of higher education in India; roll of the UGC, Finance India

CHAPTER: 3
UNIVERSITY DEVELOPMENT IN INDIA

3.1 Genesis and Early History

HISTORICALLY, the development of 'University' in India, as understood today, is round about 152 years old, the first ones having been established by the British Government in 1857 – one each at Bombay, Calcutta and Madras – along the lines of the then London University. Even for the famous Universities of Oxford and Cambridge in England, from where the idea of University and its customs were brought to India, the examples were the Universities of Paris and Bologna, the 'Progenitors' of the Universities. Hence, for a proper study of the University development, it becomes necessary that at least a brief historical reference of the **origin and development 'University' in Europe be given.**

The beginning of 'University' of today can be traced in the twelfth-thirteenth century Europe, when the role of Church, as a religious institution, was important particularly the struggle against the high-handedness of the Church Authorities. School at Cathedrals came into being in 1179 following a degree issued by the Third Lateran Council, that all secular Cathedrals should have a master to teach Clerks and poor Scholars. Persons, thus trained, were to be granted the approval of the Bishop as Teachers for the purpose of teaching, within the Cathedral precincts. But the Chancellor, as an officer of the Bishop, who was empowered to sanction license "to teach", grew so strong that he could exert the power of 'veto' and sometimes be 'venal' and sometimes, would even refuse to issue license to anyone who considered "un-orthodox".

Such high-handedness of the chancellor gradually germinated discontent among the masters and a stage came when the teachers of masters in such great Cathedral Schools as, Notre Dame in Paris organized themselves with a self-protecting guild or Universities. Came thus into being the 'university of masters'. Paris is thus, the example of Oxford and Cambridge. Bologna, a free city in a northern Italy, was the other originator of the idea of University which had the 'University of Students'. These two originators of University ideas had distinctive features. For example, while Paris had its, 'gild of masters', Bologna had the 'gild of students'. Further, while Paris had the reputation for studies in theology, Bologna was pre-eminent in both Civil and Canon law. Bologna which had its gild of students, appointed their own Rector, hired and paid their teachers and also decided their courses of studies, while in Italy, during the course of time, more universities grew up or four Reggio, Pedua, Siena, etc. Over about a period of three or four centuries, the rule for students was replaced by the control of masters.

The universities thus came into being through the conjunction of so many factors as growth of the Cathedrals, the initiative of the city state, the welcoming charity of monasteries, the brilliance and reputation of teachers like Aberald and John of Salisbury, the interest of the Pope and the King.

3.2 Concept of University

The concept of university can be put to two tests.

a) The First Test:

According to Rashdall, the 'University' is a body of 'teachers or scholars', but not a 'place'.

b) The Second Test:

Newman has, on the contrary, attached importance to the 'place' which attracted students of every kind.

Rashdall definition seems to be more correct. After all, a student, when he moves out to seek knowledge, should able to drink it from the fountain of knowledge of the teachers. Fundamentally, therefore, to the students, the test of 'University' is the body of 'Teachers or Scholars'.

The second Test is 'a place', which attracts students of 'every kind'. This, by itself, is an implied corroboration of the first test as in order to attract students to transmit knowledge, for which alone the students will flock at a place the presence of the body of 'Teachers or Scholars' is a pre-requisite. Nevertheless, since the Scholars or Teachers have to have, 'a place' where the students could flock studies of various subjects for fuller development of their faculties, even the second test is maintainable – but only in the context of the first test.

Hence, the word 'University' refers the existence of a corporate body of Teachers or Scholars, a place, where the students would be attracted to drink freely from the fountain of knowledge, provided by the teachers and, of course, finally grant 'licenses' to the worthy students at the end of the successful completion of the Courses of Studies.

3.3 The modern meaning of the word 'University':

An institution organized and incorporated for the purpose of imparting instruction, examining students, and otherwise promoting education in the higher branches of literature, scie nce, art, etc., empowered to confer degrees in the several arts and faculties, as in theology, law, medicine, music, etc. A university may exist without having any college connected with it, or it may consist of but one college, or it may comprise an assemblage of colleges established in any place, with professors for instructing students in the sciences and other branches of learning.

3.4 Earlier Systems and Institutions – A Comparison

In India, the position was different as advocated by Prof. H.D.Sankalia. Even from the Upanisadic times, it had evolved a system of education which could stand comparison, in so far as the essentials are concerned, with similar organizations of the West, known as 'City Schools', 'Stadium General', 'University' etc. In course of time, that system was found prevalent in the Ashramas, Mathas and Viharas.

Essentials of a University, as Hastings Rashdall has maintained, were present in India from time of Buddhist institutions which flourished mainly at Taxila, Nalanda, and Vikramsila. Although Nalanda dates back far before the Christian era, it did not reach the state of glory before the rise of Mahayana Buddhism, at the beginning of the Christian era. Its reputation attracted scholars in the fourth century. Rashdall further maintains that the real ingredients of University, as are acceptable to us, appeared in Europe only from the twelfth and thirteenth centuries. He does not recognize the institutions prior to this period as those having the necessary features of the University.

Prof. H. D. Sankalia opined that, in view of the system and organization needed for a University, in India, it could only be a Buddhist Sangha and to some extent Jaina as the nucleus of a University and not a Hindu or Brahmin Ashrama of a Rishi. But Radha Kumud Mookerji holds that the essential ingredient of the Buddhist Education was but a phase of the ancient Hindu or Brahminical System of education.

3.5 The First Universities

With the support of Aukland, Bentinck and Raja Ram Mohan Roy, the principles of education was shaped in the famous Dispatch of the Court of Directors sent to the Governor-General in India on the 19th July, 1854, which inter-alia led to the establishment of the first Universities in India, viz. University of Bombay, University of Calcutta, University of Madras along the lines of the then University of London. Although three separate Acts were passed and brought into force on 24th

January, 1857 for the University of Calcutta, 18th July, 1857 for the university of Bombay and 5th September, 1857 for the University of Madras, they actually started functioning from 1858.

Under the act of these first modern Indian Universities, they were to be managed by a Chancellor and a Senate consisting of a Vice-Chancellor and the Fellows to be appointed by the Government. The functions of the Universities were to confer degrees to the candidates who met the requirements, as laid down by the Universities. They were to promote liberal education and senior scholarship and to regulate the studies so as to equip the students in different professions in life.

Of the three Presidency Universities, while the University of Bombay and the University of Madras were to have their Governors as Chancellors, in the case of the Calcutta University, the Governor-General was the Chancellor. As regards jurisdiction, Bombay served the old Bombay province comprising Sindh, Gujarat, Kathiawar (Saurashtra), Karnatak (without Mysore) as well as Maharastra excluding VIdarbha; Madras covered the whole of the Southern Region. In the case of the Calcutta University, its jurisdiction extended over the rest of India (as it was then) and from Rangoon to Peshwar.

Initially the type of these Universities was affiliating. To begin with, they had four Departments viz., Arts-cum-Sciences, Law, Medicine and Engineering.

An organized system of higher education was thus introduced in India through the establishment of the three Universities. This at once boosted the pace of development of higher education and consequently more colleges came into being enrolling larger number of students. Following the incentives flowed from the Education Dispatch of 1854, the missionary efforts contributed significantly to the expansion of higher education. Impact of such activities, particularly when combined ones of Roman Catholic and Protestant missionaries were taken into account together they "…. exceeded the government output in education remarkably" for they were "...pleased to see legal sanction added to their activities as a result of the recommendations of the Education Dispatch of 1854."

However, on account of the Government's subsequent policy of 'strict neutrality' towards religion, as a result of the proclamation issued by the Queen Victoria, after India was declared part of the British Empire, to the Princes. Chiefs and people of India, the support and assistance that the missionaries were so far receiving following the recommendation of the Education Dispatch of 1854, ceased to flow from the Government resulting in sharp decline in the expansion of education both school and collegiate

Table 3.1: Universities established in the pre-independence period

Sr. No.	University	Year of establishment
1.	University of Calcutta, Calcutta.	1857 (January)
2.	University of Bombay, Bombay.	1857 (January)

3.	University of Madras, Madras.	1857 (September)
4.	Punjab University, Lahore. (now named as Lahore University).	1882
5.	University of Allahabad, Allahabad.	1887
6.	Banaras Hindu University, Varanasi.	1916
7.	Mysore University, Mysore.	
8.	Patna University, Patna.	1917
9.	Osmania University, Hyderabad.	1918
10.	Aligarh Muslim University, Aligarh.	1920
11.	Lucknow University. Lucknow.	1920
12.	University of Dacca.	1920
13.	University of Delhi, Delhi.	1920
14.	University of Nagpur, Nagpur.	1923
15.	Andhra University, Waltair.	1926

16.	University of Agra, Agra.	1927
17.	Annamalai University, Annamalainagar.	1929
18.	University of Kerala, Kerala.	1937
19.	Utkal University, Bhuvaneswar.	1943
20.	University of Saugar, Sagar.	1946
21.	University of Rajasthan, Jaipur.	1947 (January)

3.6 Universities in Post-Independence Period

In the post-independence period, for a variety of reasons, growth the universities was rapid, the first being the Punjab University, Chandigarh. The Punjab University was already established in the undivided India, at Lahore, in 1882, which covered the East Punjab as well.

With the division of India and Lahore, being the head-quarters of the Punjab University falling in the area of the newly created Pakistan, Punjab University had to take re-birth on the divided Indian soil with its headquarter at Chandigarh. It came into being, as a result of promulgation of an Ordinance on the 27th September, 1947 setting up the East Punjab University with effect from October 1, 1947. The Ordinance was later replaced on November 16,1947 by the East Punjab University Act of 1947.

Since there was already the Punjab University functioning at Lahore, the name of the new University at Chandigarh had to be made, for the purpose of its proper identity, as the East Punjab University. It is now known as the Punjab University and the original Punjab University at Lahore is now known as the Lahore University.

Growth of Universities was rather fast in the post-independence period for a variety of reasons. In 1949 alone, four universities came into being – Roorkee, Poona, M.S. University of Baroda and Karnatak. In all 100 new Universties have been established in the post independence period, bringing the total number of 119.

3.7 Specialized Universities

One of the significant characteristics of the new Universities established in the post-independence period is that some are for specialized studies which make a departure from the traditional concept that Universities which meant 'universality of subjects'. The university of Roorkee was established in 1949, from a college of Engineering which has Faculties of Engineering, Science and Architecture. Similarly, more Universities of Special characters have also been established e.g. India Kala Sangit Vishwavidyalaya, exclusively devoted to Music and Fine Arts at Khairagarh in Madhya Pradesh, Varaneseya Sanskrit Vishwavidyalaya (now Sampurnanand Sanskrit Vishwavidyalaya) for Oriental Learning, Agricultural Universities in various States for Agricultural Sciences and Technology, the Kameshwar Singh Darbhanga Sanskrit Vishwavidyalaya in Bihar for the traditional Sanskrit Learning, the Rabindra Bharati Univrsity in Calcutta mainly as a University for Dance, Drama and Music and also in Humanities, the Gujarat Ayurveda University, Jamnagar, for the teaching of Ayurveda, the traditional Indian system of medicine.

3.8 Specialized Institutions of Higher Learning

Yet another significant new characteristic found in the post-independence period is that, in addition to the Universities of special characters created after 1947, the Government of India has accepted and recognized a number of institutions of Higher Learning in two distinctive categories.

a) Institutions recognized as Deemed to be Universities

These institutions are recognized by the university Grants Commission under section 3 of its Act, as 'Deemed Universities'. Most of these institutions were originally established long before the University Grants Commission came into being in 1956. For example, the Gurukul Kangri Vishwavidyalaya was established in 1900. Indian Agricultural Research Institute in 1905, and the Indian Institute of Science in 1909. The University Grants Commission, however, recognized all these institutions during the period from 1958 to 1981.

Table 3.2 List of Some of the Institutions recognized 'Deemed Universities' after Independence

Sr. No.	Name of Institutions
1.	Birla Institute of Technology and Science, Pilani.
2.	Central Institute of English and Foreign Languages, Hyderabad.
3.	Gujarat Vidyapith, Hyderabad.
4.	Gurukul Kangri Vishwavidyalaya, Haridwar.
5.	Gandhigram Rural Institute, Madurai.
6.	Indian Agricultural Research Institute, New Delhi.
7.	Indian Institute of Science, Bangalore.
8.	Indian School of Mines, Dhanbad.
9.	Jamia Millia Islamia, New Delhi.
10.	Tata Institute of Social Sciences, Bombay
11.	School of Planning and Architecture, New Delhi.
12.	Dayalbagh Educational Institute, Agra
13.	Shri Satya Sai Institute of Higher Learning, Anantapur.
14.	Bharati Vidyapeeth, Pune

b) Institutions of National Importance

These institutions were later declared as institute of National Importance in the Acts enacted by the Parliament. The table 3.3 will show the list of these institutions. Except the All India Institute of Medical Sciences, all the institutions were in existence from before ranging from two to fifty two years and were later declared as institutions of National Importance in the Acts enacted by the Parliament. The All-India Institute of Medical Sciences has been declared as an Institution of National Importance from the year of its inception i.e. 1956.

Table 3.3 List of Institutions of National Importance

Sr. No.	Name of Institutions
1.	All India Institute of Medical Sciences, New Delhi.
2.	Dekshin Bharat Hindi Prachar Sabha, Hyderabad.
3.	Indian Institute of Technology, Mumbai.

4.	Indian Institute of Technology, New Delhi.
5.	Indian Institute of Technology, Kanpur.
6.	Indian Institute of Technology, Madras.
7.	Indian Institute of Technology, Kharagpur.
8.	Indian Statistical Institute, Calcutta.
9.	Post-Graduate Institute Medical Education, Chandigarh,
10.	Indian Institution of Guwahati.
11.	Shree Chitra Tirunal Institute of Medical Sciences and Technology, Thirunvananthapuram.
12.	Indian Institute of Technology, Roorkee.
13.	National Institute of Pharmaceutical Education and Research, Mohali (Punjab).

3.9 Open University

In the modern innovative world of learning, the Open University has surely broken new grounds to provide education to those who have interest and ability to continue their education and study in there 'own time' which has been greatly appreciated and welcomed all over the world. The unique features of the open university system is that no formal academic qualification is required for admission to under-graduate course.

The idea of Open University was first mooted and implemented in U.K. in January, 1969. The university is also known as the University of the Air (by which title the project was originally known).

The Open University System was initiated in the country to augment opportunities for higher education as an instrument of democratizing education and also to make it a lifelong process. The first Open University in the country was established by the state government of Andhra Pradesh in 1982. In 1985, the central government established the Indira Gandhi National Open University (IGNOU).

Through the open universities and distance learning initiatives, mechanisms are in place to upgrade skills at regular intervals and develop new competencies. People's needs of lifelong learning are constantly expanding. Higher education institutions are offering learning opportunities to satisfy these diverse demands. Ready access and flexibility are the hallmarks of these initiatives. At present there are fourteen Open Universities in India.

3.10 Introduction of Study Unit – Saurashtra University

Saurashtra University, Rajkot (Gujarat), a State University was established on May 23, 1967. In November 1968, the University was recognized under 2 (f) and 12 (b) of the UGC Act of 1956. It is a teaching cum affiliating university.

The history of the Saurashtra University goes back to 1953 when two great Gandhian philosophers and devoted educationists of Gujarat, Late Dolarrai Mankad and Late Harbhai Trivedi, published a book stressing the need for a separate university for Saurashtra region. As a result of continued all round support for this proposal, the Government of Gujarat established Saurashtra University with the motto ' Let our learning be purifying' and also 'Let the Goddess of Learning (Saraswathi) make us pure through her knowledge'. The University aims at establishing itself as a financially sound and academically vibrant institution of international repute. Another importance attached to this area is that the Father of the Nation – Mahatma Gandhi – had his early education in Rajkot.

Saurashtra University has a vast and nice campus of 410 acres, situated in the city of Rajkot. The University is located in a backward region of Gujarat and has been catering mainly to the needs of first generation learners in the field of higher education. The University has 25 departments in various disciplines of Arts, Science, Commerce, Business Administration, Law, Education and Computer Science. The University is offering 25 P.G programmes, 4 M.Phil. programmes, 19 Ph.D. programmes, 25 Under-graduate Programmes besides many Diploma, Certificate and Post- Doctoral programmes in different disciplines. The University has 154 affiliated colleges catering to the needs of rural Saurashtra. There are 111 permanent teachers of whom 86 are Ph.D.holders, and the rest are either M.Phil. or Master Degree holders. The number of non-teaching staff is 429. The student enrolment for PG, M.Phil and Ph.D Programmes stands at 6235, 103 and 343 respectively as on 2009. The student population for under-graduate programme is 92,301 including 3876 from other states in the current academic year. There are 71 PG Centres functioning in colleges affiliated to the University.

The University has a reasonably good infrastructure. The teaching programmes are conducted under annual system though, some courses are taught under semester scheme.

CHAPTER: 4
ANALYSIS OF DATA

4.1 Meaning of not-for-profit organizations

- Not-for-Profit organizations refer to those organizations which:

- are formed for the purpose of promoting commerce, art, science, religion, charity or any other useful object.

- Intend to spend their income in promoting their objectives, and

The examples of such organizations include Sports Clubs, Social Clubs, Public Libraries, Charitable Hospitals, Educational Institutions, Temples, Churches, Gurudwaras. Masjids and Professional bodies (e.g., The Institute of Chartered Accountants of India. The Institute of Cost and Works Accountants of India. The Institute of Company Secretaries of India).

Such entities may or may not have trading activities. If trading activities are carried on by such entities, then the profit arising therefrom is used for the purpose of promoting the objectives for which such entities were formed. For example, if a sports club also runs a restaurant, the profit of such a restaurant is used to promote the service objectives.

It may be noted that the restriction is on the application of income and not on the earning of income by not-for-profit organizations.

4.2 FUND BASED ACCOUNTING
Meaning

Fund theory calls for fund based accounting rather than entity based accounting (which is done in case of profit seeking organizations).

Fund based accounting essentially involves preparation of financial statements fundwise and consolidation of those statement to represent the financial results/position of the organization as a whole.

According to Governmental Accounting Standards Boards, USA Codification of Governmental Accounting and Financial Reporting Standards, A fund may be defined as an accounting entity "with a self-balancing set of accounts regarding cash and/or other resources together with all related liabilities and residual equities or balances, and changes therein, which is segregated for the purpose of carrying specific activities of attaining certain objectives in accordance with special regulations, restrictions of limitations". Thus, every fund is aimed at fulfilling some purpose and the services embodied in the assets are the primary means to achieve that purpose.

The accounting for these not-for-profit entities is primarily based on the fund theory. The fund theory is based on the following equation :

Assets = Restrictions on Assets

Assets represent prospective services to the fund and liabilities represent restrictions against the assets of the fund. For example, in case of a university, the most commonly used specific funds are endowment funds, development funds etc. Each of these funds has its specific assets restricted for particular purposes. Under the fund theory, the balance sheet is considered an 'inventory statement' of assets and those restrictions applicable to the assets.

In fund-based accounting, the following statements are to be prepared to get a consolidated picture of the organization as a whole:

1. Income and Expenditure Account for each of the Revenue Funds. (Whether restricted or Unrestricted) or Statement of Activity.
2. Statement showing changes in Balance of each Fund [Whether Revenue Fund or Specific Fund]
3. Balance Sheet of each of the Funds [Whether Revenue Fund or Specific Fund]
4. General Balance Sheet of the organization as a whole

Some academics argue that the income and expenditure account should better be called 'Statement of activity' A not-for-profit organization may have no income other than grants and gifts received from government and well wishers. In that situation, it is proper to name the statement showing the normal revenue operations of the organization as the statement of Activity. But in case of educational institutions like Schools, Colleges or universities, fees from students form a significant portion of revenue receipts. Therefore, we can continue to call the Statement of Activity as income and Expenditure Account.

Classification of Funds

Funds may be classified as follows:

1. Revenue Fund
2. Capital Fund / Special Fund

4.3 Explanation of Revenue and Capital Sources of Income and Expenditure of Saurashtra University

In the **revenue fund income sources**, the income of Saurashtra university is divided in to 12 heads of income. The heads are:-

1. Tuitions and Other Fees of Post Graduate

Tuitions and other fees of Post Graduate include department wise income of 24 department and tuition fees from colleges.

2. Exam Fees

Exam Fees include examination fees from 24 departments and in addition, Convocation charges, marksheet verification fees, miscellaneous income and re-assessment fee.

3. University Library

The head of university library includes income from fine, waste paper-Sale, library fee from P.G. Department, other income :zerox etc., and recovery of books price.

4. University Publication

University Publication includes income received from publication published by the university.

5. University Hostel

University Hostel head includes income from girls and boys who are using the facility of hostel.

6. Estate

Estate includes income from guest house, rent, and water electricity income.

7. Other Fees

The Other Fees head includes enrolment fee, registration fee of graduate and post graduate, eligibility fee, migration and other certificate fee, and affiliation fee.

8. State Government Maintenance Grants

This head includes grant received yearly from state government which is by nature non plan grant, revenue income and is used for the maintenance of university and to meet its yearly revenue expenditure.

9. Miscellaneous Income

This head includes income from waste paper sale, other income etc.

The remaining heads of revenue income are:-

10. Continuing Education

11. Package deal Recovery

13. Bonus Grant

In the Revenue Fund Expenditure sources the expenditure of Saurashtra university is divided into 23 heads of expenditure. The heads are:-

1. Post Graduate Education and Research Expenditure

This head is divided into 3 sub expenditure which are:-

a. **Post graduate department expenditure** which includes department wise expenditure of 24 departments.

b. **Post graduate centre colleges** which includes expenditure like remuneration and traveling allowance to P.G. teachers, Chemical glassware, library expenses, administrative expenses, scholarship and free ships, and studies and tours.

c. **Scholarship** expenditure means scholarship provided to the students of P.G. department.

2. Examination Expenses

This head includes expenses of examination of individual department regarding paper setting and examining, question paper printing expense, traveling allowance to paper setters and examiners, supervision charges, conduct expense at exam centre, answer books, stationery, and cyclostyle expense, remuneration given for practical exams, expenses of chemical and equipment for practical exam, printing expense, coding, decoding, mark sheet preparation charge, postage and telegram, exam staff traveling allowance, convocation expenditure, exam honorarium to staff, central assessment, computer expenditure, traveling allowance to observers, contingency vehicle telephone etc., reassessment expenditure, and temporary staff pay.

3. Library Expenses

This head includes expenses like purchase of books, subscriptions of periodicals, books and periodicals binding, printing and stationery, contingency, computerization expense, and furniture and equipment repairing.

4. University Publication

This head includes expenditure done for the publication of university.

5. Hostel Expenses

This head includes expenses like contingency, boys hostel contingency, and girls hostel contingency.

6. Estate Section Expense (including guest house expense)

This head includes expenses like water supply, garden expenditure, motor car maintenance, furniture and equipment repairing, electricity and maintenance, contingency, road and building maintenance, electricity and water contingency, guest house maintenance, electronics security system and maintenance, and guest house maintenance.

7. Continuing Education Centre

This head includes expenses of two types which are contingency (stats.) and printing expenses (socio.).

8. Salary Expenditure of University Employees

This head includes salary of

a) Vice Chancellor

b) Pro Vice Chancellor

c) Registrar

d) C.E.O.

e) P. G. department Administrative Staff

f) Library Staff

g) P.G. Dept. Teachers

h) Health Centre

i) Hostel

It also includes under the heads of each pay, special pay, dearness allowance, house rent allowance, compensatory local allowance, medical allowance, provident fund and gratuity, transport allowance, temporary staff pay etc. as per the materiality principle.

9. Administrative Expenditure

It includes in it expenditure of

a) Vice Chancellor Office

b) Pro. Vice Chancellor Office

c) Allowance

d) Registrar Office

It also includes under the head of it the list of expenditure done by the university like telephone, traveling expenses, etc. as per the materiality principle.

10. Physical Education

This head includes expenses like inter zonal and inter university competition, traveling expenses, training camps, yoga camps, and maintenance expenses of sports ground.

11. Student Welfare Activities

This head includes expenses like office expenses and student welfare aid, student delegate tour expense, cultural activities camps, and adventurous activities expense

12. Health Centre

This head includes expenses like medicines and miscellaneous expenses, medical reimbursement, contingency, visiting expert doctors, and equipments for pathology laboratory,

13. Computer Centre

This head includes expenses like computer maintenance and service of equipment, updating of computer centre equipment and software, contingency provision, postage and telegram, stationery and consumable, and caution money deposit.

The remaining heads of revenue expenditure are:-

14. Department of Journalism

15. Higher Grade Scale Arrears

16. Extra Co-curricular activities

17. Leave Travel Concession

18. Adhoc Bonus

19. Pension

20. Encashment of Leave

21. Maintenance of Building

22. Vth Pay Commission Arrears

23. Expenditure of Capital Nature

As the income of non profit organization is divided into two heads revenue fund and capital fund by nature.

Now, Let us study the **capital fund income and Expenditure** of Saurashtra university. As the Capital fund income received is for a specific purpose its expenditure is also done for that specific purpose.

The capital fund income and expenditure source of saurahstra university is divided into 5 heads which are as follows:-

1. Grant from U.G.C.

This head includes grant which is planned and is capital by nature. It includes all together 83 subheads for which U.G.C. has provided grant to Saurashtra university. The number of Sub head may differ as per its utilization. This number is of the year 2003-2004.

2. Grant from State Government

This head includes grant which is planned and is capital by nature. It includes all together 14 subheads for which state government has provided grant to Saurashtra University. The number of Sub head may differ as per its utilization. This number is of the year 2003-2004.

3. Grant from Others

This head includes grant received from others for a particular purpose, it is also planned grant and is capital by nature. It includes all together 82 subhead for which it has received grant from others. The number of Sub head may differ as per its utilization. This number is of the year 2003-2004.

4. Donation and Endownment

This head includes the donation and endownment received from donors by the university. It is also planned grant and is capital by nature. It includes all together 181 subhead for which it has received donation and endowment from donors. The number of Sub head may differ as per its utilization. This number is of the year 2003-2004.

Some times the grants shows the under utilization and some times it shows over utilization of it.

5. Other Fund

This head includes the fund that university has by creating fund like:-

4.4 Analysis of Revenue Income aspect by Common Size Method

Revenue fund income sources of university in common size form is presented in table 4.0 Before starting analysis let us know about the criteria the researcher has decided to know about the share of individual heads in total income or expenditure.

Table 4.1

Explaining criteria for type of share in total revenue income expenditure

Criteria of highest point share	Type of Share
up to 0.09%	negligible share
From 0.10% to 15.00%	Minor share
From 16.00% to 45.00%	average share
from 46% to 70%	Major share

The table that is framed above is framed for the convenience of the researcher to find out about the important heads of income and expenditure. It is not a standard table. Again its range is fixed after looking at the share of different heads in common size and it is framed in such a manner that most of the important heads are covered.

Below the analysis of the same as per individual heads of revenue income

Tuition and other fees of post graduates share in total revenue income lies in between 2.02% to 7.24% in the overall research period that is from 1996-97 to 2004-05. From table 4.1 it emerges that, tuition and other fees of post graduates has the highest point share in total income in the year 2004-05 when it is accounted by 7.24% and it was at the lowest point in the year 2003-04 when it is accounted by 2.02%. Its relative share however throughout the year shows a fluctuating trend. **Tuition and other fees of post graduates covers minor share in university total revenue income.**

Chart 4a

Tuitions and Other Fees of Post Graduate Share in

Total Revenue Income

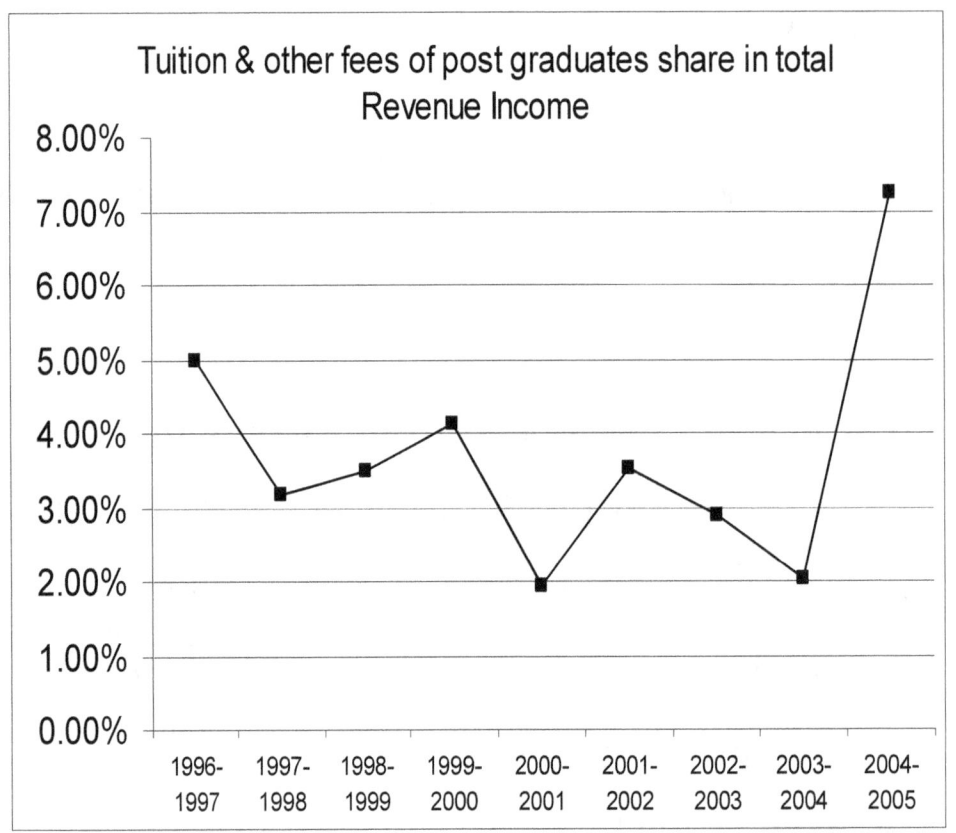

From the chart 4a given above it is seen that the share of tuition and other fees of post graduates give a fluctuating trend. It is 5% in 1996-97 after that it has shown a decreasing trend compare to 1996-97 in each years else in 2004-05 when it has reached a share of 7.24%, which is its highest point.

Exam Fees share in total revenue income lies in between 21% to 32% in the overall research period that is from 1996-97 to 2004-05. From table 4.1 it emerges that, Exam Fees has the highest point share in total income in the year 2003-04 when it is accounted by 32.65% and it was at the lowest point in the year 2000-01 when it is accounted by 21.07%. Its relative share however throughout the year shows a fluctuating trend. Normally its share rotates in between 21% to 23% during the year 1996-97 to 2001-02, than it increased by overall 9% in the next two years that is 2002-04. Than in 2004-05 its share against got reduced to 29.78%. **Exam Fees covers average share in university total revenue income.**

Chart 4b

Exam Fees Share in Total Revenue Income

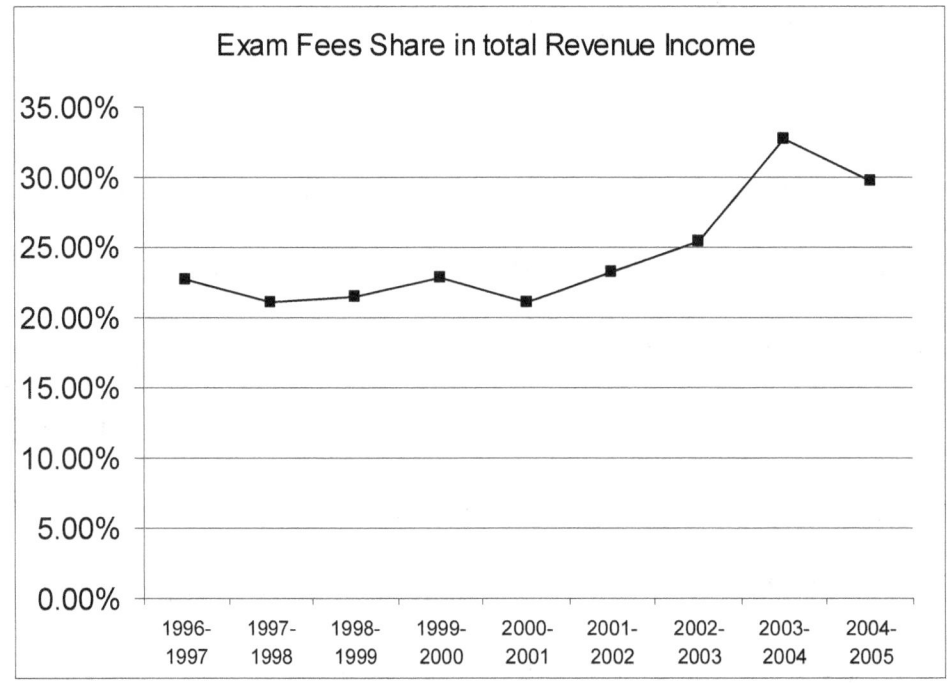

From the chart 4b we can see that as compared to the year 1996-97 the exam fees has reduced from 1997-99 by -0.02% and -0.01%. It is equivalent to base year in 1999-00. Then comparing with base year it got reduced by -0.02% in 2000-01. After that it increased in the year 2001-05 by 0.01% in 2001-02, 0.03% in 2002-03, 0.10% in 2003-04 and in 2004-05 by 0.07%. The fluctuation in exam fee income is minute as comparing its share with total revenue income.

University Library Fees share in total revenue income lies in between 0.21% to 0.30% in the overall research period that is from 1996-97 to 2004-05. From table 4.1 it emerges that, University Library Fees has the highest point share in total income in the year 1998-99 when it is accounted by 0.30% and it was at the lowest point in the year 1997-98 when it is accounted by 0.21%. Its relative share however throughout the year shows a fluctuating trend. **University Library Fees income covers minute share in university total revenue income.**

University Publication share in total revenue income lies in between 0.00% to 0.03% in the overall research period that is from 1996-97 to 2004-05. From table 4.1 it emerges that, University Publication has the highest point share in total income in the year 1999-00 when it is accounted by 0.03% and it is nil in the year 2002-03 when it accounted by 0.00%. Its relative share however throughout the year shows a fluctuating trend and the shape of its trend will be reverse of U shape curve. **University publication income covers negligible share in university total revenue income.**

University Hostel share in total revenue income lies in between 0.01% to 0.21% in the overall research period that is from 1996-97 to 2004-05. From table 4.1 it emerges that, University Hostel has the highest point share in total income in the year 2004-2005 when it is accounted by 0.21% and it was at the lowest point in the year 2003-04 when it is accounted by 0.01%. Its relative share however throughout the year shows a fluctuating trend. **University Hostel Income covers minute share in university total revenue income.**

Estate Income share in total revenue income lies in between 0.06% to 0.29% in the overall research period that is from 1996-97 to 2004-05. From table 4.1 it emerges that, Estate Income has the highest point share in total income in the year 2004-05 when it is accounted by 0.29% and it was at the lowest point in the year 1998-99 and 1999-00 when it is accounted by 0.06%. Its relative share however throughout the year shows a fluctuating trend. **University Estate Income covers minute share in university total revenue income.**

Continuing Education Income share in total revenue income lies in between 0.00% to 0.09% in the overall research period that is from 1996-97 to 2004-05. From table 4.1 it emerges that, Continuing Education Income has the highest point share in total income in the year 2004-05 when it is accounted by 0.09% and it is nil in the year 2003-04 when it accounted by 0.00% and it is at the lowest point share in the year 2002-03 when it is accounted by 0.01%. Its relative share however throughout the year shows a fluctuating trend. Continuing Education Income **covers minute share in university total revenue income.**

Other Fees share in total revenue income lies in between 1.98% to 4.40% in the overall research period that is from 1996-97 to 2004-05. From table 4.1 it emerges that, Other Fees has the highest point share in total income in the year 2004-2005 when it was accounted by 4.14%, and it was at the negative point in the year 2000-01 when it was accounted by -0.22% again, it was at the lowest point share in the year 1996-97 when it accounted by 1.98%. Its relative share however from the period 1996-97 to 1999-00 shows an increasing trend than, it became negative in 2000-01 by -0.22% after that in the coming years it shows a fluctuating trend. **Other Fees Income covers minor share in university total revenue income.**

Chart 4c

Other Fees Share in Total Revenue Income

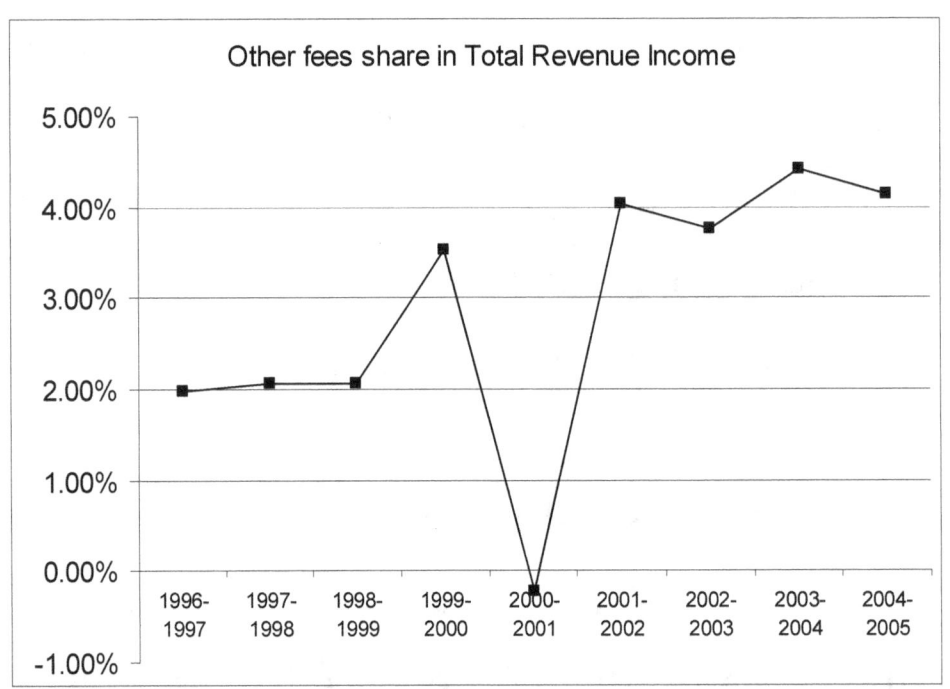

From the chart 4c we can see that as compared to the year 1996-97 the other fees has increased from 1997-99 by 0.08% equivalently. It increased by 1.56% in

1999-00. Then it was negative by -2.20% in 2000-01. After being negative it climb to 4.00% in the year 2001-02 and an increase by 2.05% as compared to the year 1996-97. Then it increased by 1.79% in 2002-03, 2.42% in 2003-04 and in 2004-05 by 2.16%. There are high up and downs in other fees income in the research period. Basically, it has climbed first in 1999-00 than a high reduction in 2000-01 and after that again climbing in the coming years.

State Government Maintenance Grant share in total revenue income lies in between 56.06% to 76.12% in the overall research period that is from 1996-97 to 2004-05. From table 4.1 it emerges that, State Government Maintenance Grant has the highest point share in total income in the year 2000-2001 when it was accounted by 76.12%, and it was at the lowest point share in the year 2004-05 when it was accounted by 56.06%. Its relative share however from the period 1996-97 to 1998-99 shows an increasing trend than, it shows fluctuating trend from 1999-00 to 2000-01 after that in the coming years that is from 2001-05 it shows a decreasing   trend. **State Government Maintenance Grant covers major share in university total revenue income.**

From the chart 4d we can see that as compared to the year 1996-97 the State government maintenance grant share has increased from 1997-99 by 0.03% equivalently. It is equivalent to base year in 1999-00. Then comparing with base year it got increased by 0.08% in 2000-01. After that it decreased in the year 2001-05 by -0.01% in 2001-02, -0.02% in 2002-03, -0.10% in 2003-04 and in 2004-05 by -0.12%. **The fluctuation in state government maintenance grant income is minute as comparing its share with total revenue income but if we compare the same in amount than the difference is high.**

Chart 4d

State Government Maintenance Grant Share in Total Revenue Income

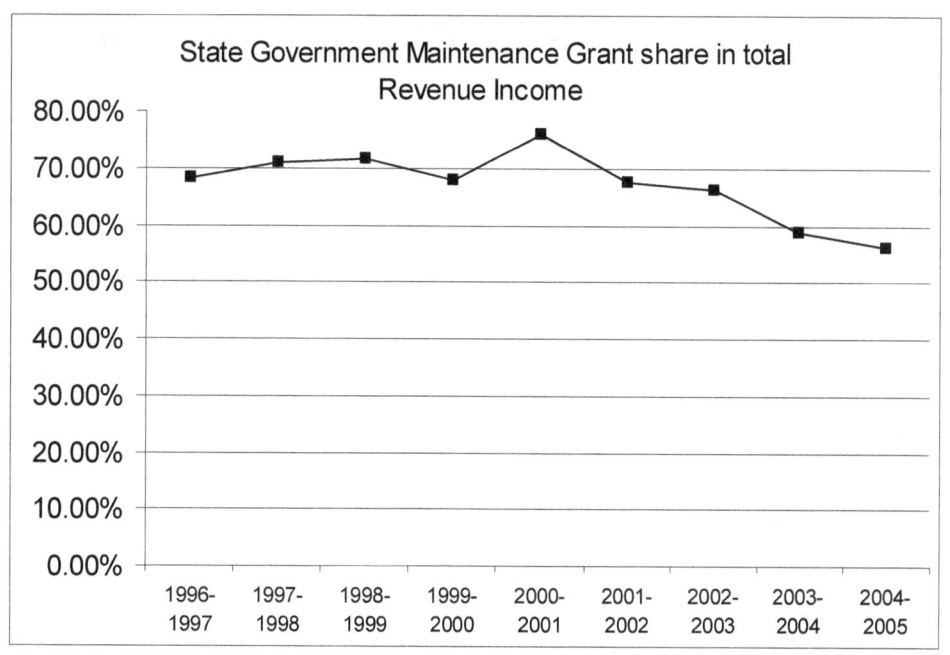

Miscellaneous Income share in total revenue income lies in between 0.36% to 1.30% in the overall research period that is from 1996-97 to 2004-05. From table 4.1 it emerges that, Miscellaneous Income has the highest point share in total income in the year 2004-2005 when it is accounted by 1.30% and it was at the lowest point in the year 2000-01 when it is accounted by 0.36%. Its relative share however throughout the year shows a fluctuating trend. **Miscellaneous Income covers minute share in university total revenue income.**

Package Deal Recovery share in total revenue income lie in between -0.03% to 0.66% in the overall research period that is from 1996-97 to 2004-05. From table 4.1 it emerges that, University Hostel has the highest point share in total income in the year 2003-2004 when it is accounted by 0.66% and it was negative in the year 1997-98 by -0.03% again it was at the lowest point in the year 1998-99 when it is accounted by 0.02%. Its relative share however throughout the year shows a fluctuating trend. **Package Deal Recovery covers negligible share in university total revenue income.**

Bonus Grants share in 1997-98 is 0.97%, else in all other years it is 0.00%. Bonus Grants share covers negligible share in university total revenue income and that also in only one year that is 1997-98.

4.5 Analysis of Revenue Expenditure Aspect in Common Size Form

Revenue fund Expenditure sources of university in common size form is presented in table 4.2. Now the analysis of the Same heading wise.

Post Graduate Education and Research Expense share in total revenue expenditure lies in between 4.54% to 11.52% in the overall research period that is from 1996-97 to 2004-05. From table 4.2 it emerges that, Post Graduate Education and Research Expense has the highest point share in total expenditure in the year 2004-05 when it is accounted by 11.52% and it was at the lowest point in the year 2000-01 when it is accounted by 4.54%. Its relative share however throughout the year shows a fluctuating trend. **Post Graduate Education and Research Expense covers minor share in university total revenue expenditure.**

Chart 4e Post Graduate Education & Research Share in Total Revenue Expenditure

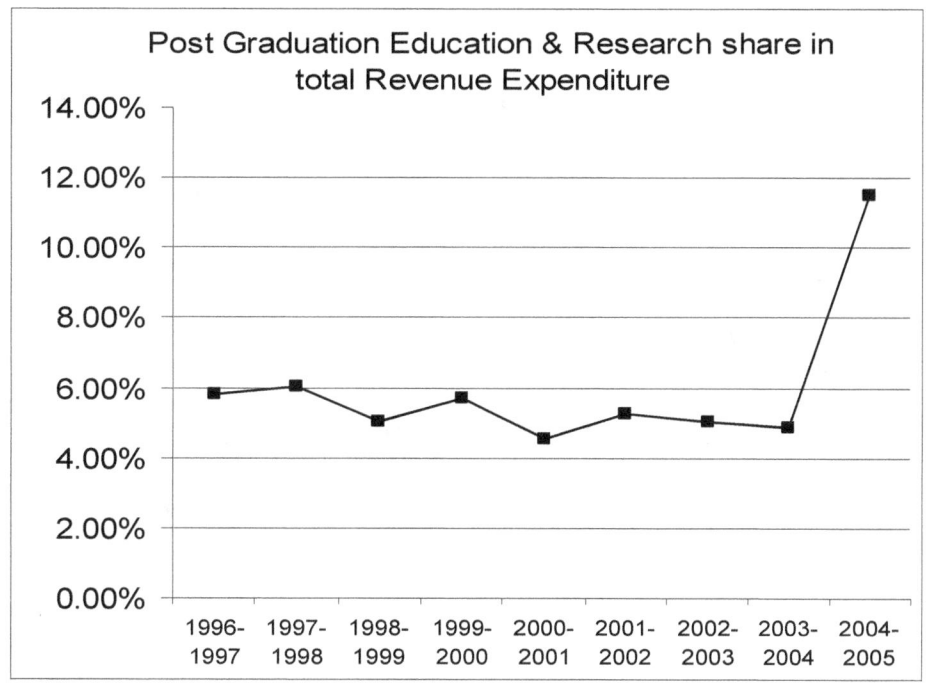

In the chart 4e given above it is clear that the difference in post graduation expenses as compared to the base year 1996-97 is minute that means it moves hardly between -0.57% to +0.23%. The change is high only in 2004-05 that is by 5.70%.

Examination Expenses share in total revenue expenditure lies in between 17.35% to 26.98% in the overall research period that is from 1996-97 to 2004-05. From table 4.2 it emerges that, Examination Expenses has the highest point share in total expenditure in the year 2003-04 when it is accounted by 26.98% and it was at the lowest point in the year 1998-99 when it is accounted by 17.35%. Its relative share however throughout the year shows a fluctuating trend. Normally its share shows a decreasing trend from the year 1996-97 to 2000-01, after that it shows an increasing trend from the year 2001 to 2003, than for 2004-05 it is reduced to 26.73%. **Examination Expense covers average share in university total revenue expenditure.**

Chart 4f

Examination Expense Share in Total Revenue Expenditure

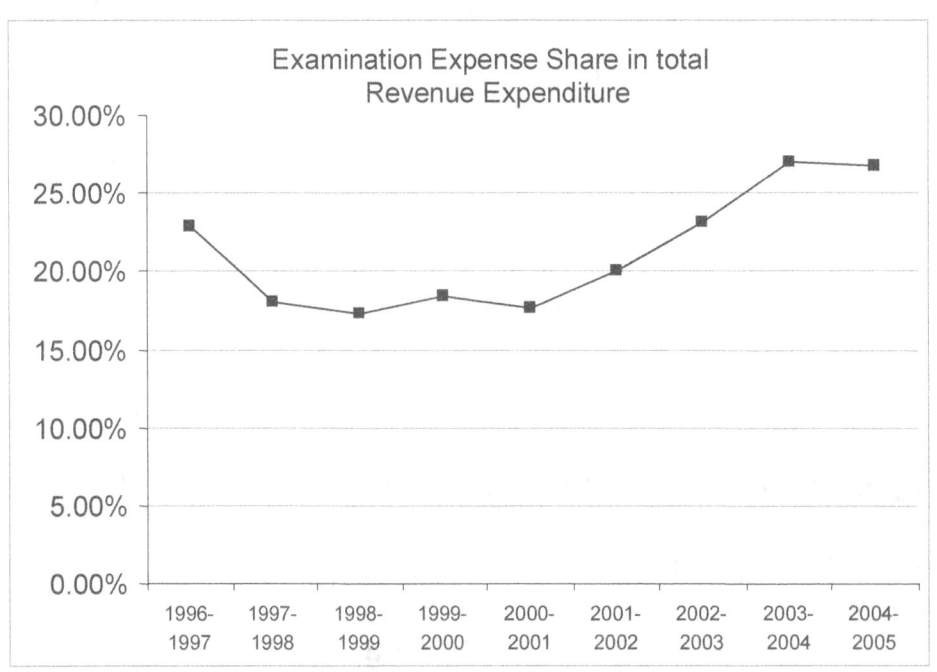

As per the chart 4f given above it is seen that examination expense share shows a declining trend from the year 1996-97 to 2001-02 and its decline rotates in between -5.60 to -2.87%. As compare to the base year the expenditure declined by -4.85% in 1997-98, -5.60% in 1998-99, -4.51% in 1999-00, -5.28% in 2000-01, and by -2.87% in 2001-02. After that it shows an increasing trend which rotates in between 0.16% to 4.03%. As compare to base year the expenditure increases in the year 2002-03 by 0.16%, 2003-04 by 4.03% and in 2004-05 by 3.78%. As it covers average share in total expenditure its declining share plays a huge role.

Library Expense share in total revenue expenditure lies in between 0.66% to 1.26% in the overall research period that is from 1996-97 to 2004-05. From table 4.2 it emerges that, Library Expense has the highest point share in total expenditure in the year 1999-00 when it is accounted by 1.26% and it was at the lowest point in the year 2004-05 when it is accounted by 0.66%. Its relative share however throughout the year shows a fluctuating trend. **Library Expense covers minute share in university total revenue expenditure.**

University Publication Expense share in total revenue expenditure lies in between 0.00% to 0.01% in the overall research period that is from 1996-97 to 2004-05. From table 4.2 it emerges that, University Publication Expense share in total expenditure in the year 1996-97 and in 2003-04 is accounted by 0.01% and for the remaining years it is 0.00%. **University Publication Expense covers negligible share in university total income.**

Hostel Expense share in total revenue expenditure lies in between 0.01% to 0.35% in the overall research period that is from 1996-97 to 2004-05. From table 4.2 it emerges that, Hostel Expense has the highest point share in total expenditure in the year 1998-99 when it is accounted by 0.35% and it was at the lowest point in the year from 2001 to 2003 when it is accounted by 0.01%. Its relative share however from the year 1996-97 to 1999-2000 shows a fluctuating trend from 0.21% to

0.35%, but from 2001-02 to 2004-05 it has reduced a lot to 0.01% to 0.03%. It has reduced totally by 97% from 1996-97 to 2004-05. **Hostel Expense covers minute share in university total revenue expenditure.**

Estate Expense share in total revenue expenditure lies in between 1.60% to 4.77% in the overall research period that is from 1996-97 to 2004-05. From table 4.2 it emerges that, Estate Expense has the highest point share in total expenditure in the year 2001-02 when it is accounted by 4.77% and it was at the lowest point in the year 1998-99 when it is accounted by 1.60%. Its relative share however throughout the year shows a fluctuating trend. **Estate Expense covers minor share in university total revenue expenditure.**

Continuing Education Centre share in total revenue expenditure lies in between 0.00% to 0.13% in the overall research period that is from 1996-97 to 2004-05. From table 4.2 it emerges that, Continuing Education Centre has the highest point share in total expenditure in the year 1999-00 when it is accounted by 0.13% and it was at the lowest point in the year 2000-01 when it is accounted by 0.02% and it is 0.00% in 2003-04. Its relative share however throughout the year shows a fluctuating trend. **Continuing Education Centre covers negligible share in university total revenue expenditure.**

Salary Expenditure of University Employees share in total revenue expenditure lies in between 49.76% to 61.93% in the overall research period that is from 1996-97 to 2004-05. From table 4.2 it emerges that, Salary Expenditure of University Employees has the highest point share in total expenditure in the year 1996-97 when it is accounted by 61.93% and it was at the lowest point in the year 2004-05 when it is accounted by 49.76%. Its relative share however throughout the year shows a decreasing trend else in the year 1998-99. As compared to 1996-97 the total salary expenditure is reduced by 12.17%. The salary expenditure of university employees as compared to 1996-97 shows reduction by 1.14% in 1997-98, 0.47% in 1998-99, 0.35% in 1999-00, 6.82% in 2000-01, 4.83% in 2001-02, 8.26% in 2002-03,

6.79% in 2003-04 and 12.17% in 2004-05. It has reduced totally by 20% from 1996-97 to 2004-05. **Salary Expenditure of University Employees covers major share in university total revenue expenditure.**

As per the chart 4g given below it is seen that salary expenditure share shows a very minute fluctuating trend and its trend rotates in between -1.39 to 2.04%. As compare to the base year the expenditure increases by 2.04% in 1997-98, and 0.40% in 1998-99. After that it shows a declining trend which rotates in between -0.28% to -1.39%. As compare to base year the expenditure declines by -0.28% in 1999-00, -1.39% in 2000-01, and by -0.30% in 2001-02. Again salary expenditure increases in 2002-03 by 0.51%, 2003-04 by 0.10% and a decline in 2004-05 by -0.53%. **As compare to the share of salary expenditure of university the fluctuations in it are very minute and normally it is seemed as a steady trend.**

Chart 4g

Salary Expenditure of university employees Share in Total Revenue Expenditure

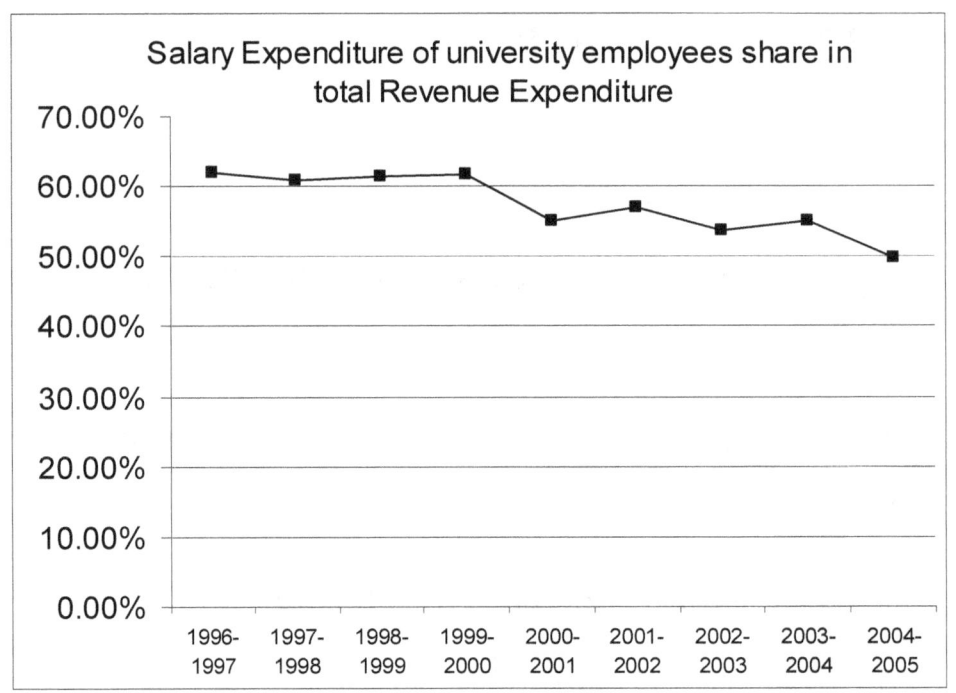

Administrative Expenditure share in total revenue expenditure lies in between 3.10% to 6.53% in the overall research period that is from 1996-97 to 2004-05. From table 4.2 it emerges that, Administrative Expenditure has the highest point share in total expenditure in the year 1997-98 when it is accounted by 6.53% and it was at the lowest point in the year 2000-01 when it is accounted by 3.10%. Its relative share however throughout the year shows a fluctuating trend.

Administrative Expenditure covers minor share in university total revenue expenditure.

As per the chart 4h given below it is seen that administrative expenditure expense share shows a very minute fluctuating trend and its trend rotates in between -1.39 to 2.04%. As compare to the base year the expenditure increases by 2.04% in 1997-98, and 0.40% in 1998-99. After that it shows a declining trend which rotates in between -0.28% to -1.39%. As compare to base year the expenditure declines by -0.28% in 1999-00, -1.39% in 2000-01, and by -0.30% in 2001-02. Again administrative expenditure increases in 2002-03 by 0.51%, 2003-04 by 0.10% and a decline in 2004-05 by -0.53%. **The increase or decrease rate in administrative expenditure is very minute.**

Chart 4h

Administrative Expenditure Share in Total Revenue Expenditure

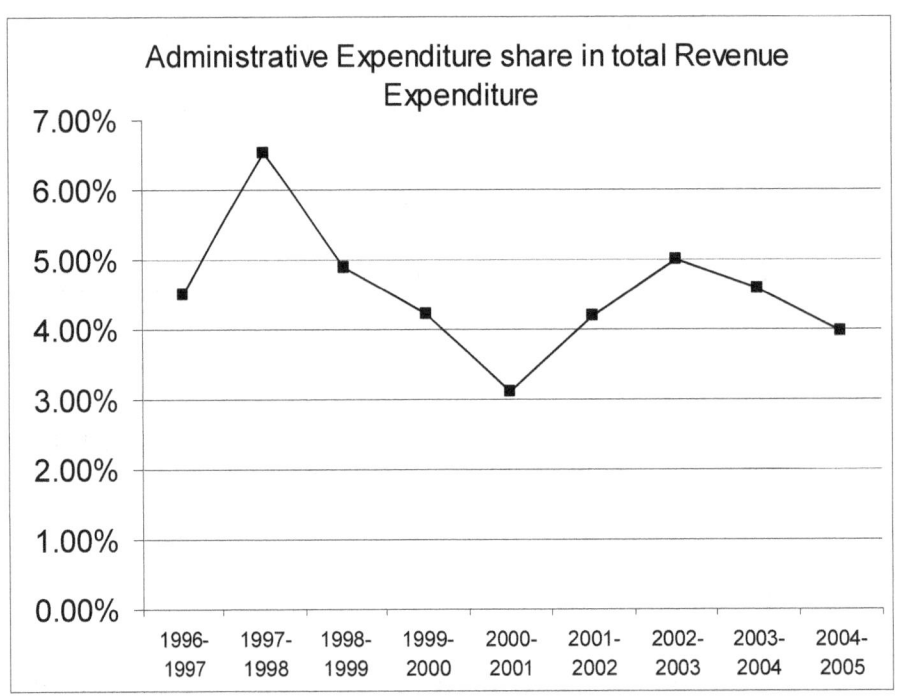

Physical Education Expenditure share in total revenue expenditure lies in between 0.28% to 2.97% in the overall research period that is from 1996-97 to 2004-05. From table 4.2 it emerges that, Physical Education Expenditure has the highest point share in total expenditure in the year 2002-03 when it is accounted by 2.97% and it was at the lowest point in the year 2004-05 when it is accounted by 0.28%. Its relative share however throughout the year shows a fluctuating trend. **Physical**

Education Expenditure covers minute share in university total revenue expenditure.

Student Welfare Activities Expenditure share in total revenue expenditure lies in between 0.08% to 0.55% in the overall research period that is from 1996-97 to 2004-05. From table 4.2 it emerges that, Student Welfare Activities Expenditure has the highest point share in total expenditure in the year 2003-04 when it is accounted by 0.55% and it was at the lowest point in the years 1998-00 when it is accounted by 0.08%. Its relative share however throughout the year shows a fluctuating trend. **Student Welfare Activities Expenditure covers minute share in university total revenue expenditure.**

Health Centre Expenditure share in total revenue expenditure lies in between 0.57% to 1.20% in the overall research period that is from 1996-97 to 2004-05. From table 4.2 it emerges that, Health Centre Expenditure has the highest point share in total expenditure in the year 1997-98 when it is accounted by 1.20% and it was at the lowest point in the year 2000-01 when it is accounted by 0.57%. Its relative share however throughout the year shows a fluctuating trend. **Health Centre Expenditure covers minute share in university total revenue expenditure.**

Computer Centre Expenditure share in total revenue expenditure lies in between 0.03% to 0.47% in the overall research period that is from 1996-97 to 2004-05. From table 4.2 it emerges that, Computer Centre Expenditure has the highest point share in total expenditure in the year 2002-03 when it is accounted by 0.47% and it was at the lowest point in the year 2004-05 when it is accounted by 0.03%. Its relative share however throughout the year shows a fluctuating trend. **Computer Centre Expenditure covers minute share in university total revenue expenditure.**

Department of Journalism expenditure has been shown in individual head of total expenditure for only one year that is 2000-01 by 0.32%. After that it has been shown in the head of Post Graduation Education and Research Expenditure.

Higher Grade Scale Arrears is only done for the years 1999-00, 2000-01 and 2002-03 by 0.09%, 0.02% and 0.02%. Higher Grade Scale Arrears covers minute share in university total revenue expenditure, again the expenditure is done only in 3 years stated above for all other years it is 0.00% of total revenue expenditure.

Extra Co-Curricular Activities expenditure is only done for one year that is 2002-03 by 0.01%, else for all other years it 0.00% of total revenue expenditure.

Leave Travel Concession share in total revenue expenditure lies in between 0.01% to 1.05% in the overall research period that is from 1996-97 to 2004-05. From table 4.2 it emerges that, Leave Travel Concession has the highest point share in total expenditure in the year 1999-00 when it is accounted by 1.05% and it was at the lowest point in the years 2003-05 when it is accounted by 0.01%. Its relative share however throughout the year shows a fluctuating trend. **Leave Travel Concession covers minute share in university total revenue expenditure.**

Adhoc Bonus share in total revenue expenditure lies in between 0.00% to 1.18% in the overall research period that is from 1996-97 to 2004-05. From table 4.2 it emerges that, Adhoc Bonus has the highest point share in total expenditure in the year 1997-98 when it is accounted by 1.18% and it was at the lowest point in the years 2004-05 when it is accounted by 0.01%. Its relative share however throughout the year shows a fluctuating trend. **Adhoc Bonus covers minute share in university total revenue expenditure.**

Encashment of Leave share in total revenue expenditure lies in between 0.00% to 2.00% in the overall research period that is from 1996-97 to 2004-05. From table 4.2 it emerges that, Encashment of Leave has the highest point share in total expenditure in the year 2001-02 when it is accounted by 2.00% and it was at the lowest point in the years 2004-05 when it is accounted by 1.25%. Its relative share however throughout the year shows a fluctuating trend. **Encashment of Leave covers minute share in university total revenue expenditure.**

Maintenance of Building expenditure is only done for one year that is 1998-99 by 0.74%, else for all other years it 0.00% of total revenue expenditure.

Vth Pay Commission Arrears share in total revenue expenditure lies in between 0.00% to 11.90% in the overall research period that is from 1996-97 to 2004-05. From table 4.2 it emerges that, Vth Pay Commission Arrears has the highest point share in total expenditure in the year 2000-01 when it is accounted by 11.90% and it was at the lowest point in the years 1999-00 when it is accounted by 0.20%. It was 0.00% for the years 1996-98. Its relative share however throughout the year shows a fluctuating trend. **Vth Pay Commission Arrears covers minute share in university total revenue expenditure.**

Expenditure of Capital Nature is only done for one year that is 1999-00 by 0.72%, else for all other years it 0.00% of total revenue expenditure.

CONCLUSION

From the analysis done above, we have come to know about the different heads occupying different position in revenue income and expenditure having different types of share like major, average, minor, minute and negligible. Now we will do further analysis of such items which cover major, average, minor and selected minute share heads only. The heads covering the same as stated above are as follows:-

a) Tuition and Other Fees of Post Graduate

b) Exam Fees

c) University Library

d) University Hostel

e) Estate

f) Other Fees

g) State Government Maintenance Grant

h) Salary of university employees

i) Administrative Expenditure

j) Health Centre Expenditure

4.5 Ratio Analysis

Ratios of different income to expenditure (All the amounts are in lakhs in all the calculations)

1. Post Graduate Department Expenditure to Income ratio

Table 4.3

Post Graduate Expenditure to Income Ratio

Year	P.G. Expenditure	P.G. Income	Ratio
1996-1997	39.57	32.44	121.96%
1997-1998	45.75	24.61	185.94%
1998-1999	49.65	34.61	143.44%
1999-2000	67.08	55.72	120.38%
2000-2001	59.79	32.43	184.37%
2001-2002	66.72	56.27	118.57%
2002-2003	72.06	51.02	141.24%
2003-2004	74.08	34.97	211.85%
2004-2005	186.85	135.54	137.86%

Post Graduate Department Expenditure to Income ratio will help us to know about **earning efficiency** of post graduate department. From Table No. 4.3 it is seen that post graduate department expenditure ratio remains high throughout the research period than its income. The ratio is at the lowest point in the year 2001-02 by 118.57% and it is at the highest point in the year 2003-04 by 211.85%. The ratio rotates in between 118.57% to 211.85%. **The post graduate department has not shown any positive contribution in turnaround strategy. Again it has become a part of profit reduction every year. It expenditure remains high than its income throughout the research period. The rotation level of expenditure is also very high.**

From the chart 4i it can be seen that as compared to the base year that is 1996-97 in which the ratio is 121.96% the ratio has increased in 1997-98 by 63.98%, in 1998-99 by 21.48%, in 1999-00 it declines by -1.58%, after that again it shows an increasing trend and in 2000-01 as compared to base year an increase by 62.41%, in 2001-02 decline by -3.39%, than an increase in 2002-03 by 19.28%, in 2003-04 by 89.89% and in 2004-5 by 15.90%.

Chart 4i

Post Graduate Department Expenditure to Income Ratio

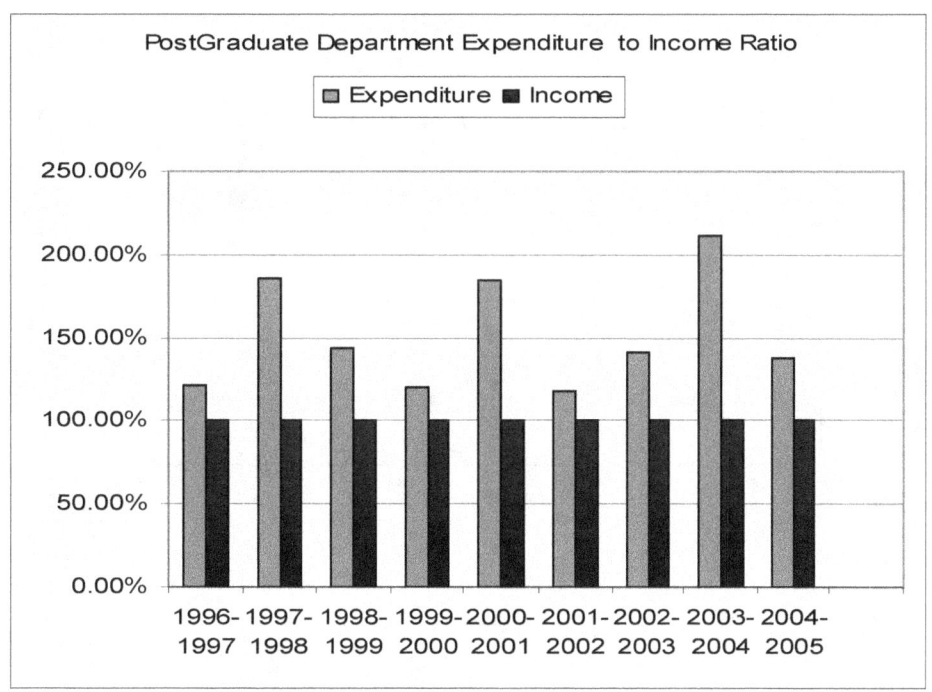

Now, the statistical analysis of the ratio using **Ttest, to check whether it remains same in all the years or not,** H_0:- There is no significant difference between Post Graduate Expenditure and Income ratio in the 9 years research period.

H_1:- There is significant difference between Post Graduate Expenditure and Income ratio in the 9 years research period.

Table 4.4

Ttest calculation and Ttest result of Post Graduate Department

Expenditure to Income ratio and Correlation Co-efficient of ratio

AVERAGE	1.52	-	-
S.D.	0.11	R^2	0.97
T_C	39.63	T_c	10.56
T_t	1.86	T_t	1.895
Result	**39.63>1.86**	**Result**	**10.56>1.895**

Here, the T_C >T_t as per table 4.4

The difference between the calculated value and tabulated value is significant so H_0 is rejected and H_1 is accepted. **That means that the ratio of Post graduate expenditure and income is not the same throughout the research period and the difference is also significant.**

The **Correlation Co-efficient** between the post graduate department expenditure and income is highly positive it is 0.97. It shows it has positive relation. If one variable increases other increases and one decreases other decreases. This is overall 9 years correlation of them.

Now, Let us apply **Ttest to check that whether the relation remains same in all years or not.**

H_0:- There is no significant difference between correlation co-efficient of Post Graduate department Expenditure and Income in the 9 years research period.

H_1:- There is significant difference between correlation co-efficient of Post Graduate department Expenditure and Income in the 9 years research period.

Here, the $T_C > T_t$ as per table 4.4

The difference between the calculated value and tabulated value is significant so H_0 is rejected and H_1 is accepted. **That means that there is significant difference between correlation co-efficient of Post Graduate department Expenditure and Income in the 9 years research period. The relation changes throughout the years due to that only the changes in the post graduate expenditure and income are not in equal proportion.**

2. Examination Expenses to Income Ratio

Table 4.5

Examination Expenditure to Income Ratio

Particulars	Expenditure	Income	Ratio	Net
1996-1997	155.89	147.83	105.45%	-8.06
1997-1998	136.80	163.54	83.64%	26.75
1998-1999	171.70	213.82	80.30%	42.12
1999-2000	217.73	307.24	70.87%	89.50
2000-2001	232.45	353.10	65.83%	120.65
2001-2002	254.95	370.48	68.82%	115.53
2002-2003	331.38	450.43	73.57%	119.06
2003-2004	409.55	564.56	72.54%	155.01
2004-2005	433.65	557.86	77.74%	124.20

Examination Expenditure to Income ratio will help us to know about **earning efficiency** of examination department. From Table No. 4.5 it is seen that examination income ratio remains high throughout the research period than its expenditure else in the year 1996-97. The ratio is at the lowest point in the year 2000-01 by 65.83% and it is at the highest point in the year 1996-97 by 105.45%. The ratio rotates in between 65.83% to 105.45%. **The Examination Expenditure to Income ratio shows positive contribution in turnaround strategy. Again it has become a part of profit sky-scraping every year. It income remains**

high than its expenditure throughout the research period else in the year 1998-99. The rotation level of expenditure is overall between 18% in the research period else in the year 1996-97 when it is high.

Chart 4j

Examination Department Expenditure to Income Ratio

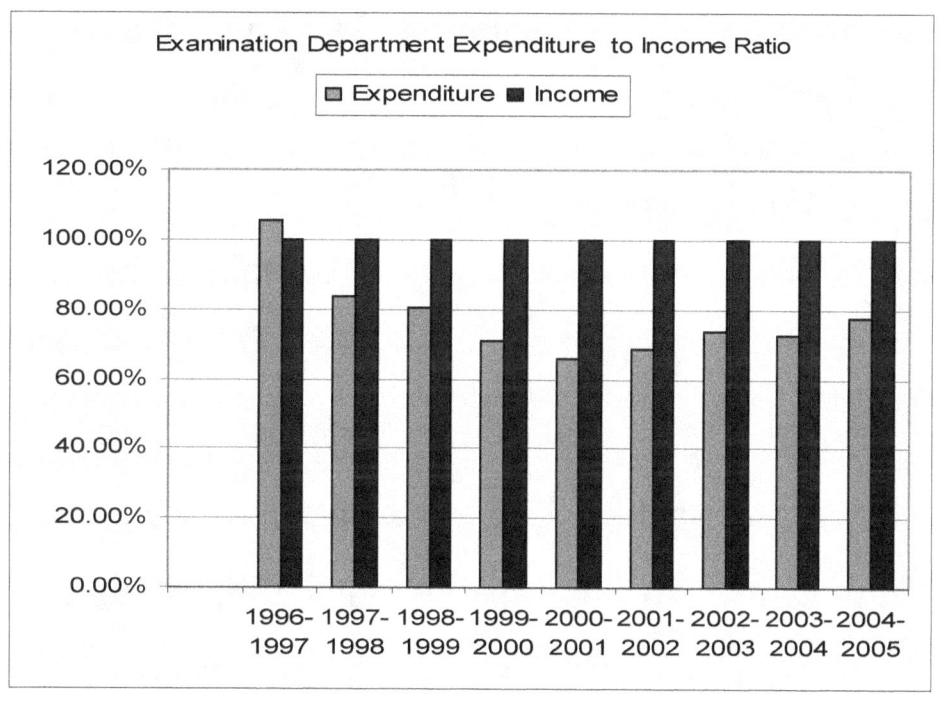

From the chart 4j it can be seen that as compared to the base year that is 1996-97 in which the ratio is 105.45% after that the expenditure has decreased throughout the years in 1997-98 by -21.81%, in 1998-99

by -25.15%, in 1999-00 by -34.58%, in 2000-01 by -39.62%, in 2001-02 by -36.63%, in 2002-03 by -31.88%, in 2003-04 by -32.91%, and in 2004-05 by -27.71%. The expenditure has reduced at the highest point in the year 2000-01 by -39.62%. The reduction of expenditure rotates between 20%.

The net surplus of the research period is given in chart 4.5. From the same we can know that the deficit in 1996-97 is by 8.06lakhs. After that there is surplus in all the years in 1997-98 by 26.75lakhs, in 1998-99 by 42.12lakhs in 1999-00 by 89.50lakhs, in 2000-01 by 120.65lakhs, in 2001-02 by 115.53lakhs, in 2002-03 by 119.06lakhs, in 2003-04 by 155.01lakhs, and in 2004-05 by 124.20lakhs. This amount is a big surplus for university. The surplus remains highest in 2003-04 by 155.01lakhs and the surplus started from 1997-98 only. Again it has become a part of profit sky-scraping every year. The following is the chart for the same.

Chart 4k

Examination Department Net Surplus Yearly

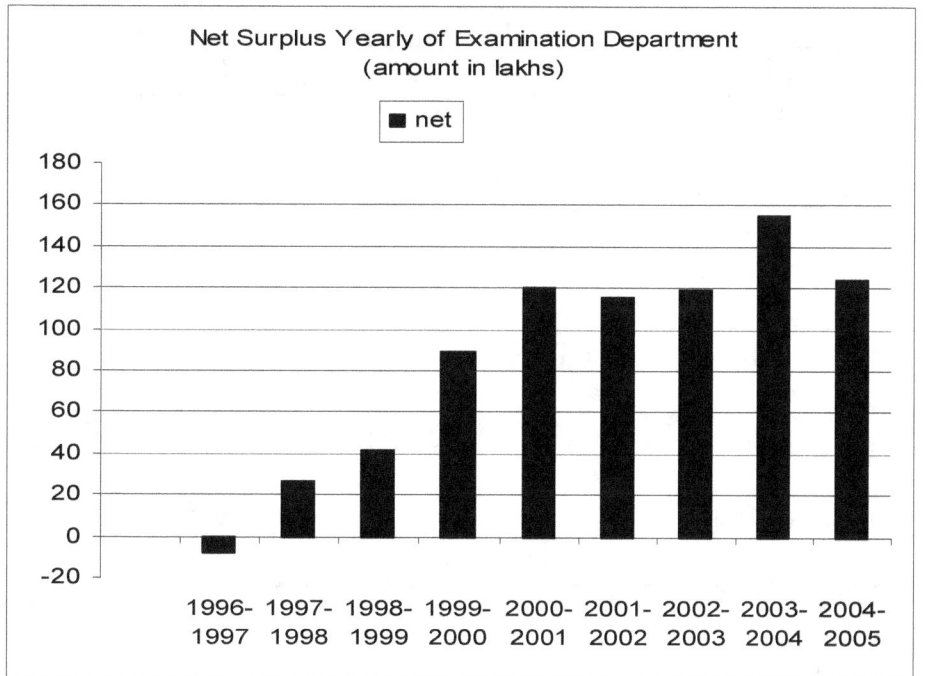

Now, the statistical analysis of the ratio using **Ttest, to check whether the ratio remains same in all the years or not,**

H_0:- There is no significant difference between Examination Department Expenditure and Income ratio in the 9 years research period.

H_1:- There is significant difference between Examination Department Expenditure and Income ratio in the 9 years research period.

Table 4.6 Ttest calculation and Ttest result of examination ratio and Correlation Co-efficient

AVERAGE	0.78	-	
S.D.	0.01	R^2	0.98
T_C	166.02	T_c	13.03
T_t	1.86	T_t	1.895
Result	**166.02>1.86**	**Result**	**13.03>1.895**

Here, the $T_C > T_t$ of ratio as per table 4.6

The difference between the calculated value and tabulated value is significant so H_0 is rejected and H_1 is accepted. **That means that the ratio of Examination Department expenditure and income is not the same throughout the research period and the difference is also significant.**

The **Correlation Co-efficient** between the post graduate department expenditure and income is highly positive it is 0.98. It shows it has positive relation. If one variable increases other increases and one decreases other decreases. This is overall 9 years correlation of them.

Now, Let us apply **Ttest to check that whether the relation remains same in all years or not.**

H_0:- There is no significant difference between correlation co-efficient of Examination department Expenditure and Income in the 9 years research period.

H_1:- There is significant difference between correlation co-efficient of Examination department Expenditure and Income in the 9 years research period.

Here, the $T_c > T_t$ of correlation coefficient as per table 4.6

The difference between the calculated value and tabulated value is significant so H_0 is rejected and H_1 is accepted. **That means that there is significant difference between correlation co-efficient of Examination department Expenditure and Income in the 9 years research period. The relation changes throughout the years due to that only the changes in the Examination expenditure and income are not in equal proportion.**

3. Library Expenditure to Income Ratio

Table 4.7

Library Expenditure to Income Ratio

Particular	Expenditure	Income	Ratio
1996-1997	4.59	1.59	288.72%
1997-1998	7.23	1.60	451.42%
1998-1999	6.98	2.96	236.16%
1999-2000	14.85	3.09	480.97%
2000-2001	12.73	3.85	330.51%
2001-2002	10.77	4.48	240.17%
2002-2003	13.29	4.07	326.27%
2003-2004	16.68	4.01	416.29%
2004-2005	10.69	4.88	219.07%

Library Expenditure to Income ratio will help us to know about **earning efficiency** of Library. From Table No. 4.7 it is seen that library expenditure ratio remains high throughout the research period than its income. The ratio is at the lowest point in the year 2004-05 by 219.07% and it is at the highest point in the year 1999-00 by 480.97%. The ratio rotates in between 219.07% to 480.97%. **The library has not shown any positive contribution in turnaround strategy. Again it has become a part of profit reduction every year. It**

expenditure remains high than its income throughout the research period. The rotation level of expenditure is also very high but the share of library expenditure and income is limited in total income and expenditure.

From the chart 41 given below it can be seen that as compared to the base year that is 1996-97 in which the ratio is 288.72% the ratio has increased in 1997-98 by 162.70%, in 1998-99 reduction by -52.56%, in 1999-00 it increase by 192.25%, in 2000-01 increase by 41.79%, in 2001-02 decline by -48.55%, than an increase in 2002-03 by 37.55%, in 2003-04 increase by 127.57% and in 2004-05 decline by 69.65%. This shows that the ratio of library expenditure to income shows fluctuating trend as compared to its base year, but it is sure that expenditure in the overall research period remains high than the income.

Chart 4l

Library Expenditure to Income Ratio

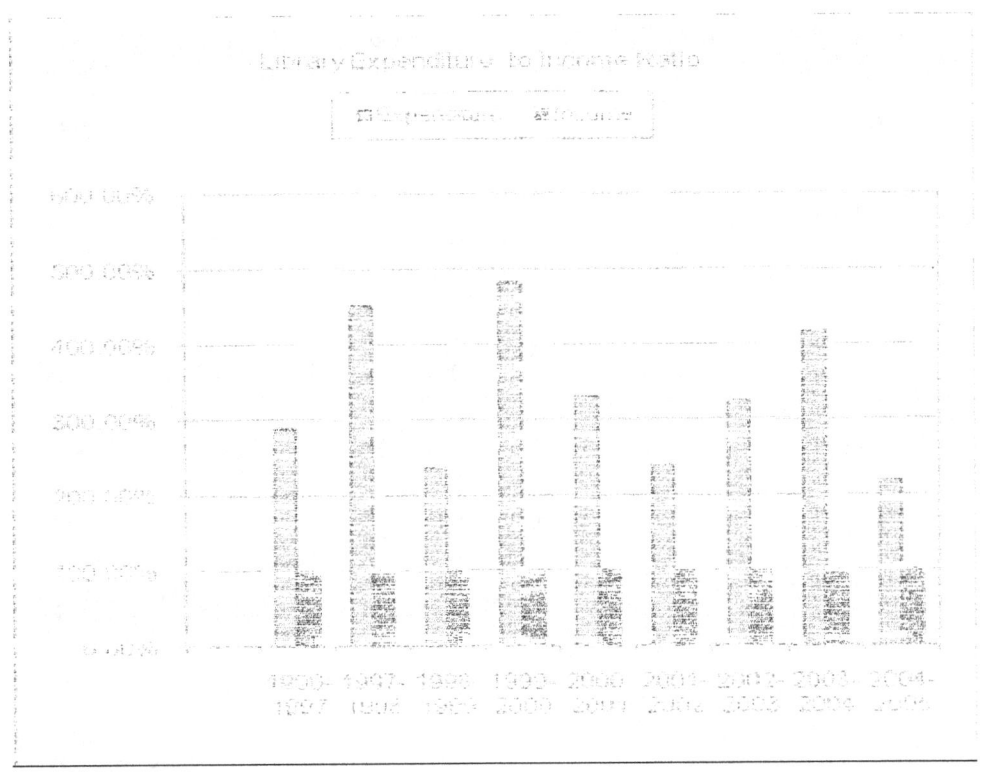

Now, the statistical analysis of the ratio using **Ttest, to check whether the ratio remains same in all the years or not,**

H_0:- There is no significant difference between Library Expenditure and Income ratio in the 9 years research period.

H_1:- There is significant difference between Library Expenditure and Income ratio in the 9 years research period.

Table 4.8 Ttest calculation and Ttest result of Library ratio and Correlation Co-efficient

AVERAGE	3.32	-	-
S.D.	0.95	r2	0.64
TC	10.51	Tc	2.20
Tt	1.86	Tt	1.895
Result	10.51>1.86	Result	2.20>1.895

Here, the $T_C > T_t$ of ratio as per table 4.8

The difference between the calculated value and tabulated value is significant so H_0 is rejected and H_1 is accepted. **That means that the ratio of Library expenditure and income is not the same throughout the research period and the difference is also significant.**

The **Correlation Co-efficient** between the Library expenditure and income is highly positive it is 0.64. It shows it has moderate positive relation. If one variable increases other increase at moderate level and if one decreases other decreases at moderate level. This is overall 9 years correlation of them.

Now, Let us apply **Ttest to check that whether the relation remains same in all years or not.**

H_0:- There is no significant difference between correlation co-efficient of Library Expenditure and Income in the 9 years research period.

H_1:- There is significant difference between correlation co-efficient of Library Expenditure and Income in the 9 years research period.

Here, the $T_C > T_t$ of correlation coefficient as per table 4.8

The difference between the calculated value and tabulated value is significant so H_0 is rejected and H_1 is accepted. **That means that there is significant difference between correlation co-efficient of Library Expenditure and Income in the 9 years research period. The correlation is moderate and again it changes throughout the years due to that only the changes in the Library expenditure and income are not in equal proportion.**

4. Hostel Expenditure to Income Ratio

Table 4.9

Hostel Expenditure to Income Ratio

Particulars	Expenditure	Income	Ratio
1996-1997	2.32	0.88	264.76%
1997-1998	2.10	0.92	229.31%
1998-1999	3.43	0.85	404.83%
1999-2000	2.44	0.58	416.72%
2000-2001	2.43	0.25	966.13%
2001-2002	0.10	1.26	7.82%
2002-2003	0.08	0.34	22.59%
2003-2004	0.36	0.25	142.10%
2004-2005	0.45	3.85	11.64%

Hostel Expenditure to Income ratio will help us to know about **earning efficiency** of hostel. From Table No. 4.9 it is seen that hostel expenditure ratio shows a fluctuating trend in the research period than its income. The ratio is at the lowest point in the year 2001-02 by 7.82% and it is at the highest point in the year 2000-01 by 416.72%. The ratio rotates in between 7.82% to 416.72%. The rotation of ratio in the research period has much ups and downs.

From the chart 4m given below it is seen that a huge expenditure has been done in hostel from the year 1996-97 to 2000-01 comparing to its income. In the years 2001-03 the hostel income is more than its expenditure. After that again in 2003-04 expenditure is high by 42.10% than income, than in 2004-05 the expenditure is just 11.64% of total income. **Hostel expenditure has shown positive as well as negative contribution in turnaround strategy. It has become a part of profit reduction for years 1996-97 to 2000-01 and in 2003-04. It has become a part of profit upliftment for years 2001-02 to 2002-03 and in 2004-05.** After doing good expenditure comparing to its income upto 2000-01 the expenditure started reducing from 2001-02 to 2002-03. Than again the expenditure are more in 2003-04 than a decline to 11.64% in 2004-05.

Chart 4m

Hostel Expenditure to Income Ratio

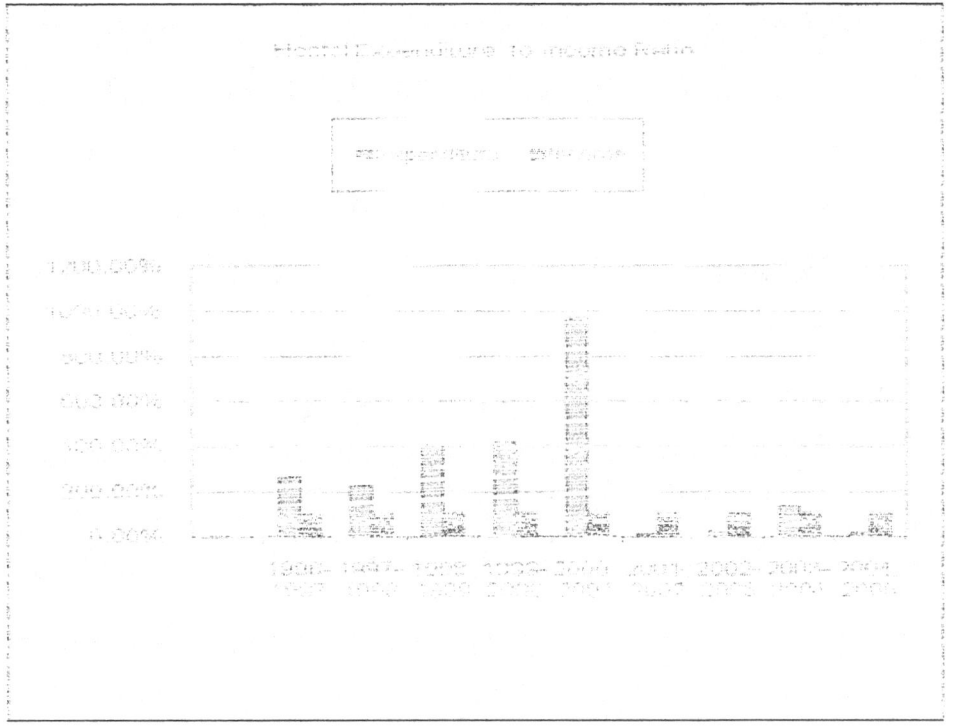

Now, the statistical analysis of the ratio using **Ttest, to check whether the ratio remains same in all the years or not,**

H_0:- There is no significant difference between Hostel Expenditure and Income ratio in the 9 years research period.

H_1:- There is significant difference between Hostel Expenditure and Income ratio in the 9 years research period.

Table 4.10 Ttest calculation and Ttest result of hostel ratio and Correlation Co-efficient

AVERAGE	2.74	-	-
S.D.	9.24	r2	-0.27
T_C	0.89	Tc	-0.74
T_t	1.86	Tt	1.895
Result	0.89<1.86	Result	-0.74<1.895

Here, the $T_C < T_t$ of ratio as per table 4.10

The difference between the calculated value and tabulated value is not significant so H_0 is accepted and H_1 is rejected. **That means that the ratio of hostel expenditure and income is same throughout the research period and the difference is not significant.**

The **Correlation Co-efficient** between the hostel expenditure and income is low negative correlation by -0.27. It shows low negative relation. If one variable increases other at low rate decreases. This is overall 9 years correlation of them.

Now, Let us apply **Ttest to check that whether the relation remains same in all years or not.**

H_0:- There is no significant difference between correlation co-efficient of hostel Expenditure and Income in the 9 years research period.

H_1:- There is significant difference between correlation co-efficient of hostel Expenditure and Income in the 9 years research period.

Here, the $T_C < T_t$ of correlation coefficient as per table 4.10

The difference between the calculated value and tabulated value is not significant so H_0 is accepted and H_1 is rejected. **That means that there is not significant difference between correlation co-efficient of Library Expenditure and Income in the 9 years research period.**

5. Estate Expenditure to Income Ratio

Table 4.11

Estate Expenditure to Income Ratio

Particulars	Expenditure	Income	Ratio
1996-1997	15.76	0.50	3164.42%
1997-1998	16.02	0.59	2703.13%
1998-1999	15.80	0.60	2615.87%
1999-2000	33.11	0.77	4317.98%
2000-2001	33.00	1.70	1942.28%
2001-2002	60.56	1.44	4216.56%
2002-2003	49.71	3.34	1487.40%
2003-2004	45.81	4.15	1104.64%
2004-2005	60.16	5.52	1090.70%

Estate Expenditure to Income ratio will help us to know about **earning efficiency** of Estate. From Table No. 4.11 it is seen that estate expenditure ratio remains heavily high throughout the research period than its income. The ratio is at the lowest point in the year 2004-05 by 1090.70% and it is at the highest point in the year 1999-00 by 4317.98%. The ratio rotates in between 1090.70% to 4317.98%. Here the expense on estate is very high as compared to its income. If we discuss in amount the income from estate is just 0.50 means

50000Rs. and the expenditure is 15.76lakh these only shows a huge difference of 1996-97. It is not so that the income has not increased but as compared to income the expenditure in the research period remains very heavily high. Huge expenditure has been done on the maintenance of estate.

As per chart 4n given below the expenditure ratio is 3164.42% in the base year that is 1996-97 after that as compared to the base year the expenditure decreases by -461.29% in 1997-98, after that by -548.55% in 1998-99, than an increase by 1153.56% in 1999-00, again decrease in 2000-01 by 1222.14%, in 2001-02 increase by 1052.14%, in 2002-03 decrease by -1677.02%, in 2003-04 decrease by 2059.78%, and in 2004-05 decrease by -2073.72%. This increase or decrease is as compared to the base year. But overall the estate expenditure remains high than its income during the research period. The expenditure done is very high in the years 1996 to 1999 and in 2001-02. It rotates in between 2073.72% to 4317.98% in this period. After that also it remains high compare to its income but not as high as in the very high expenditure period. After the very high expenditure period it rotates in between 1090.70% to 1942.28%. Normally expenditure started declining after the period 2001-02. **The estate income has also increased in the research period but not in proportion with the heavy increase in estate expenditure. University has done huge expenditure for estate maintenance as compared to its income.**

Chart 4n

Estate Expenditure to Income Ratio

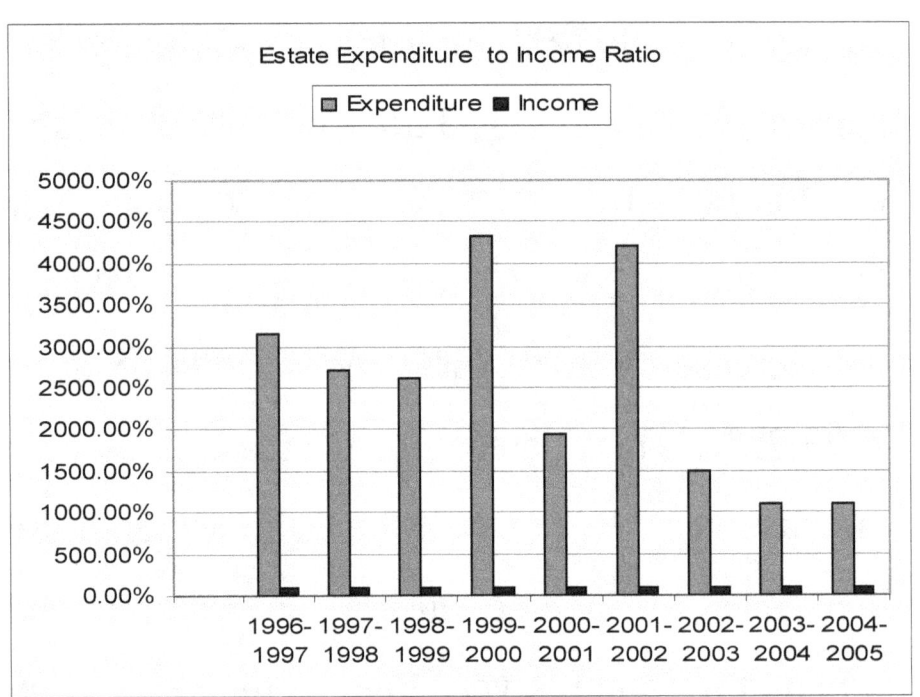

Again the Estate section loss rotates in between the amount of 15.43lakhs to 59.12lakhs. The loss remain less in the period 1996-99 and near by 15 to 16lakhs but after that it started increasing and reached up to 59.12lakhs.

This loss plays a vital role in cutting of profit of university year by year. But Estate section maintenance or development is basic requirement for university and expenditure on it is demanded time to time.

Now, the statistical analysis of the ratio using **Ttest, to check whether the ratio remains same in all the years or not,**

H_0:- There is no significant difference between Estate Department Expenditure and Income ratio in the 9 years research period.

H_1:- There is significant difference between Estate Department Expenditure and Income ratio in the 9 years research period.

Table 4.12

Ttest calculation and Ttest result of Estate ratio and Correlation Co-efficient

AVERAGE	25.16		
S.D.	150.19	r2	0.75
T_C	0.50	Tc	3.00
T_t	1.86	Tt	1.895
Result	**0.50<1.86**	**Result**	**3.00>1.895**

Here, the $T_C < T_t$ of ratio as per table 4.12

The difference between the calculated value and tabulated value is not significant so H_0 is accepted and H_1 is rejected. **That means that the ratio of Estate Department expenditure and income is same throughout the research period and the difference is also not significant.**

The **Correlation Co-efficient** between the estate expenditure and income is 0.75. It shows it has highly positive relation. If one variable increases other increases and one decreases other decreases. This is overall 9 years correlation of them.

Now, Let us apply **Ttest to check that whether the relation remains same in all years or not.**

H_0:- There is no significant difference between correlation co-efficient of Estate Expenditure and Income in the 9 years research period.

H_1:- There is significant difference between correlation co-efficient of Estate Expenditure and Income in the 9 years research period.

Here, the $T_C > T_t$ of correlation coefficient as per table 4.12

The difference between the calculated value and tabulated value is significant so H_0 is rejected and H_1 is accepted. **That means that there is significant difference between correlation co-efficient of Estate Expenditure and Income in the 9 years research period. The relation changes throughout the years due to that only the changes in the Estate expenditure and income are not in equal proportion in research period.**

6. Salary Expenditure of University Employees to State Government Maintenance Grant Ratio

Table 4.13

Salary Expenditure of University Employees to State Government Maintenance Grant Ratio

Particulars	State Govt. Maint. Grant	Ratio	balance
1996-1997	444.50	94.65%	5.35%
1997-1998	550.03	83.53%	16.47%
1998-1999	711.01	85.52%	14.48%
1999-2000	916.65	79.32%	20.68%
2000-2001	1275.66	56.83%	43.17%
2001-2002	1074.70	67.48%	32.52%
2002-2003	1173.80	65.56%	34.44%
2003-2004	1015.15	82.47%	17.53%
2004-2005	1050.00	76.87%	23.13%

Salary Expenditure of university employees is the expenditure that covers major part of university total expenditure and State Government maintenance grant is a grant that covers major part of university total income.

As per table 4.13 it is clear that the salary expenditure in all the years remains less than its maintenance grant received. In the year 1996-97 the expenditure shared 94.65% of maintenance grant, than 83.53% share in 1997-98, of grant, in 1998-99 share by 85.52%, in 1999-00 share by 79.32%, in 2000-01 share by 56.83%, in 2001-02 share by 67.48%, in 2002-03 share by 65.56%, in 2003-04 share by 82.47% after that in 2004-05 share by 76.87%. The Salary Expenditure share in the grant received shows a fluctuating trend. It remains at lowest point in the year 2001-02 by 56.93% but in the same year the grant received is maximum that is 1275.66lakhs. It remains at the highest point in the year 1996-97 by 94.65% and in this year only the grant received is minimum by 444.50lakhs. The grant rotates in between 56.83% and 94.65%. The ratio of grant is in between 56.83% to 79.32% in the years 1996-97 to 1999-2000. This years rotate is average as compared to its total research period rotate. Than in the period from 2001-2003 it rotates in between 56.83 to 65.56%. This is low rotate period as compared to its total research period. After that again it rotates in between 76.87% to 82.47%.

It is again a surprise to see that in the period of 2001-03 in which the expenditure ratio is low that is in between 56.83% to 65.56% in the same period the university has got the highest grant that is in between 1074.70 to 1275.66lakhs. After that period from 2003-05 the grant received is reduced but expenditure has been increased.

From the chart 4o it is seen that the state government grant has enough balance each year after meeting its salary expenditure. The balance is at highest point in the year 2000-2001 and it is at the lowest point in the year 1996-97. The balance rotates in between 5.35% to 43.17%.

Chart 40

Salary Expenditure to State Government Maintenance Grant Ratio and State Government Grant Net

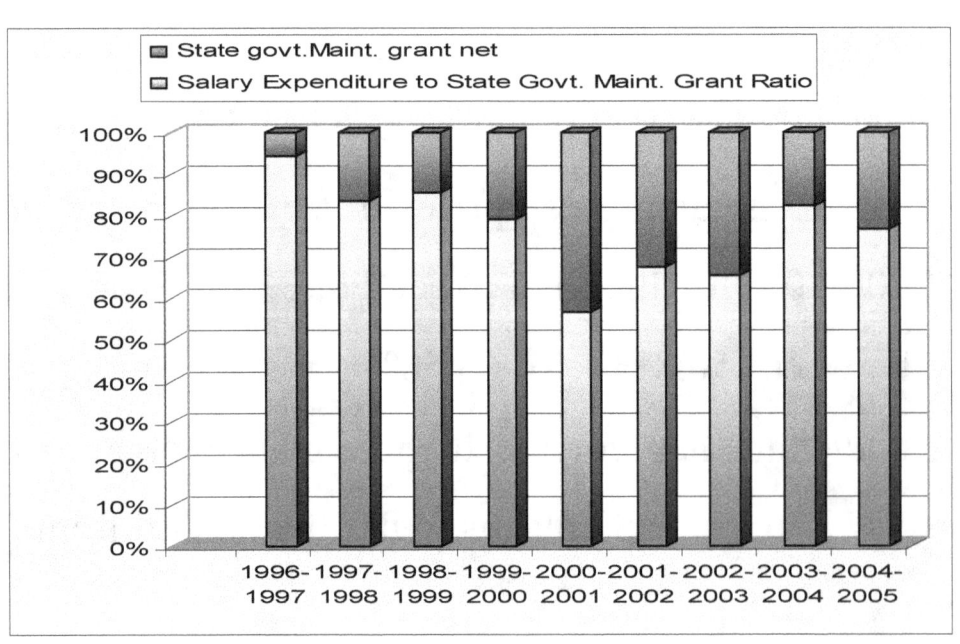

Now, the statistical analysis of the ratio using **Ttest, to check whether the ratio remains same in all the years or not,**

H_0:- There is no significant difference between Salary Expenditure of teachers and State Government Maintenance Grant ratio in the 9 years research period.

H_1:- There is significant difference between Salary Expenditure of teachers and State Government Maintenance Grant ratio in the 9 years research period.

Table 4.14 Ttest calculation and Ttest result of ratio and Correlation Co-efficient

AVERAGE	0.77	-	-
S.D.	0.01	R2	0.88
T_C	16.92	Tc	4.88
T_t	1.86	Tt	1.895
Result	16.92>1.86	**Result**	4.88>1.895

Here, the $T_C > T_t$ as per table 4.14

The difference between the calculated value and tabulated value is significant so II_0 is rejected and H_1 is accepted. **That means that the ratio of**

Salary Expenditure of teachers and State Government Maintenance Grant is not the same throughout the research period and the difference is also significant.

The **Correlation Co-efficient** between the Salary Expenditure of teachers and State Government Maintenance Grant is highly positive it is 0.88. It shows it has positive relation. If one variable increases other increases and one decreases other decreases. This is overall 9 years correlation of them.

Now, Let us apply **Ttest to check that whether the relation remains same in all years or not.**

H_0:- There is no significant difference between correlation co-efficient of Salary Expenditure of teachers and State Government Maintenance Grant in the 9 years research period.

H_1:- There is significant difference between correlation co-efficient of Salary Expenditure of teachers and State

Government Maintenance Grant in the 9 years research period.

Here, the $T_C > T_t$ as per table 4.14

The difference between the calculated value and tabulated value is significant so H_0 is rejected and H_1 is accepted. **That means that there is significant difference between correlation co-efficient of Salary Expenditure of teachers and State Government Maintenance Grant in the 9 years research period. The relation changes throughout the years due to that only the changes in the Salary Expenditure of teachers and State Government Maintenance Grant are not in equal proportion.**

7. Administrative Expenditure to State Government Maintenance Grant Ratio

Table 4.15

Administrative Expenditure to State Government Maintenance Grant Ratio

Particulars	Administrative Expenditure	State Govt. Maint. grants	Ratio	Balance
1996-1997	30.52	444.50	6.87%	413.98
1997-1998	49.39	550.03	8.98%	500.65
1998-1999	48.40	711.01	6.81%	662.62
1999-2000	49.70	916.65	5.42%	866.95
2000-2001	40.84	1275.66	3.20%	1234.82
2001-2002	53.25	1074.70	4.96%	1021.45
2002-2003	71.68	1173.80	6.11%	1102.12
2003-2004	69.72	1015.15	6.87%	945.43
2004-2005	64.26	1050.00	6.12%	985.74

From table 4.15 it is clearly seen that administrative expenditure that is the average expenditure of university covers hardly 3.20% to 8.98% of state government maintenance grant. The expenditure is at lowest point in 2000-2001 by 3.20% and in this year only maximum grant is received that is 1275.66lakhs again the expenditure is maximum in the year 1997-98 by 8.98%. The administrative expenditure rotates in between 3.20%

to 8.98%. The administrative expenditure covers a very minor share of state government maintenance grant. If we look at the expenditure amount is increasing but rise is not in proportion with the state government maintenance grant.

From the chart 4p it is clear that administrative expenditure has shown rise in amount but as compared to rise in state government grant the expenditure shows a decreasing or a steady trend. The expenditure fluctuates in between 3.80% to 8.98%. As compare to base year 1996-97 the expenditure rises by 2.11% in 1997-98, than it decreases by -0.06%,-1.44%, -3.67%, -1.91% and -0.76% from 1998-2003. After that it share is steady with the base year in 2004, after that a decline by -0.75% in 2004-05 as compared to the base year.

Chart 4p

Administrative Expenditure to State Government
Maintenance Grant Ratio

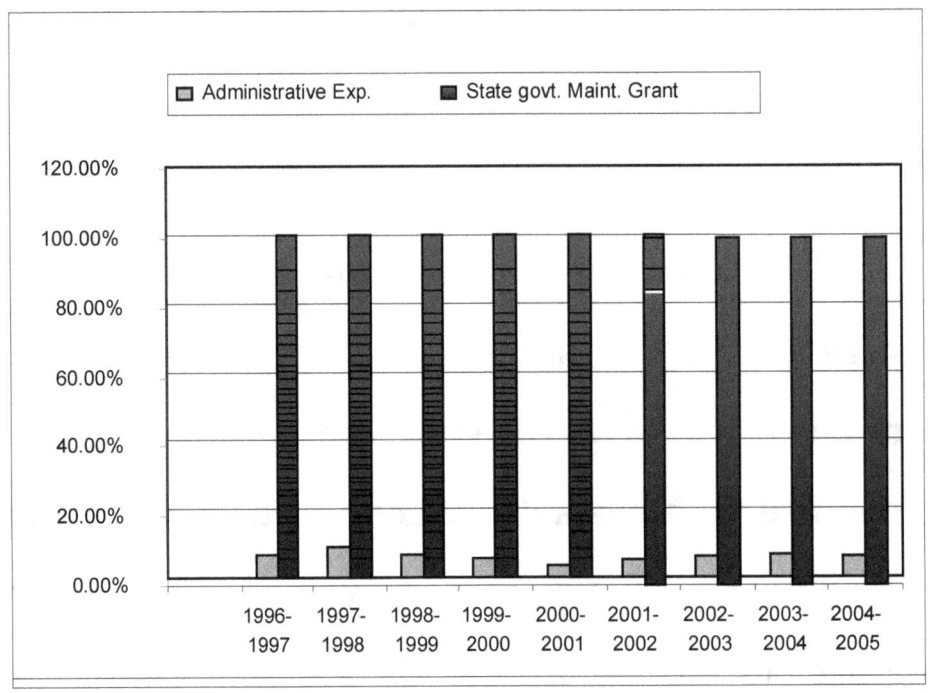

Now, the statistical analysis of the ratio using **Ttest, to check whether the ratio remains same in all the years or not,**

H_0:- There is no significant difference between Administrative Expenditure and State Government Maintenance Grant ratio in the 9 years research period.

H_1:- There is significant difference between Administrative Expenditure and State Government Maintenance Grant ratio in the 9 years research period.

Table 4.16 Ttest calculation and Ttest result of ratio and Correlation Co-efficient

AVERAGE	0.06	-	-
S.D.	0.00	R2	0.75
T_C	7.33	Tc	3.00
T_t	1.86	Tt	1.895
Result	**7.33>1.86**	**Result**	3.00>1.895

Here, the $T_C > T_t$ as per table 4.16

The difference between the calculated value and tabulated value is significant so H_0 is rejected and H_1 is accepted. **That means that the ratio of** administrative expenditure and State Government Maintenance Grant **is not the same throughout the research period and the difference is also significant.**

The **Correlation Co-efficient** between the administrative expenditure and State Government Maintenance Grant is highly positive it is 0.75. It shows it has positive relation. If one variable increases other increases and one decreases other decreases. This is overall 9 years correlation of them.

Now, Let us apply **Ttest to check that whether the relation remains same in all years or not.**

H_0:- There is no significant difference between correlation co-efficient of Administrative Expenditure and State Government Maintenance Grant in the 9 years research period.

H_1:- There is significant difference between correlation co-efficient of Administrative Expenditure and State Government Maintenance Grant in the 9 years research period.

Here, the $T_C > T_t$ as per table 4.16

The difference between the calculated value and tabulated value is significant so H_0 is rejected and H_1 is accepted. That means that there is significant difference between correlation co-efficient of Administrative Expenditure of teachers and State

Government Maintenance Grant in the 9 years research period. The relation changes throughout the years due to that only the changes in the Salary Expenditure of teachers and State Government Maintenance Grant are not in equal proportion. This shows that changes in both the items are not in equal proportion year by year.

8. Salary Expenditure + Administrative Expenditure + deficit or surplus of Post Graduate Department, Library, Hostel, Estate to State Government Maintenance Grant Ratio

Table 4.17 Total of salary expenditure, administrative expenditure and deficit/surplus of Post Graduate Department, Library, Hostel, Estate

Particulars	Salary Expenditure of university employees	Administrative Expenditure	Deficit or surplus of p.g, library, hostel, estate	Total of 1,2,3
1996-1997	420.73	30.52	26.83	478.08
1997-1998	459.45	49.39	43.39	552.22
1998-1999	608.09	48.40	36.84	693.33
1999-2000	727.07	49.70	57.32	834.09
2000-2001	724.98	40.84	69.72	835.54
2001-2002	725.17	53.25	74.70	853.12
2002-2003	769.53	71.68	76.36	917.58
2003-2004	837.18	69.72	93.56	1000.45
2004-2005	807.13	64.26	108.36	979.75

The table 4.17 shows the total of expenditure coming under the main head of university expenditure and the loss born by university under some of it heads.

Table 4.18 Total of salary expenditure, administrative expenditure and deficit/surplus of Post Graduate Department, Library, Hostel, Estate to State Government Maintenance Grant Ratio

Particulars	Total of expenditure shown (in lakhs)	S.G.M.Grants (in lakhs)	Ratio	Net Deficit/Surplus (n lakhs)
1996-1997	478.08	444.50	107.56%	-33.58
1997-1998	552.22	550.03	100.40%	-2.18
1998-1999	693.33	711.01	97.51%	17.69
1999-2000	834.09	916.65	90.99%	82.56
2000-2001	835.54	1275.66	65.50%	440.12
2001-2002	853.12	1074.70	79.38%	221.58
2002-2003	917.58	1173.80	78.17%	256.22
2003-2004	1000.45	1015.15	98.55%	14.70
2004-2005	979.75	1050.00	93.31%	70.25

From the table 4.18 it is clear that expenditure is more than the grant only in the years 1996 to 1998. After that in all the years that is from 1999 to 2005 grant is more than the total income. State Government grant is able to absorb three of its main expenditure and again it is standing with surplus in years 1999-2005. The surplus is also in lakhs. The ratio is lowest in the year 2000-01 by 65.50% and again in this year the grant received is maximum and the net surplus of income and expenditure is also maximum. The ratio is highest in the year 1996-97 by 107.56%. The Income and Expenditure loss is all maximum in the year 1996-97. The grant acquired in this year is also lowest. This proves that when grant received is minimum in proportion expenses are also high and deficit is there but in the years when grant received is maximum expenses are not high in that proportion and surplus is maximum. The total expenditure rotates in between 65.50% to 107.56%. **The expenditures are high in the years 1996-97 to 1999-00. The expenditure have shown maximum decline from the years 2001-2003. They have started rising again in the year 2004-05 comparing to decline period that is 2001-03. Here university should take care that expenditure rise should be in proportion of grant rise otherwise they might come in problem. This analysis shows that after meeting all main expenses also university has surplus, again examination surplus, other fees income and miscellaneous income is also going to be added in it although few expenditure are to be deducted from it but the share of this expenditure are minute or negligible.**

From the chart 4q you can see that after meeting all main expenditure state government maintenance grant have surplus in it in the years 1998 to 2005. The deficit is in the first two years that is 1996 and 1997. The surplus is maximum in 2000- 2001 by 401.12lakhs. From here it is seen that main turnaround period is from 1999-00 to 2002-03 after that again the surplus is there but comparatively it has started declining. And the deficit is in 1996-97 which has started reducing in 1997-98 and after that deficit getting transferred into surplus.

Chart 4q Net Deficit or Surplus of State Government Grant after meeting main 3 expenses

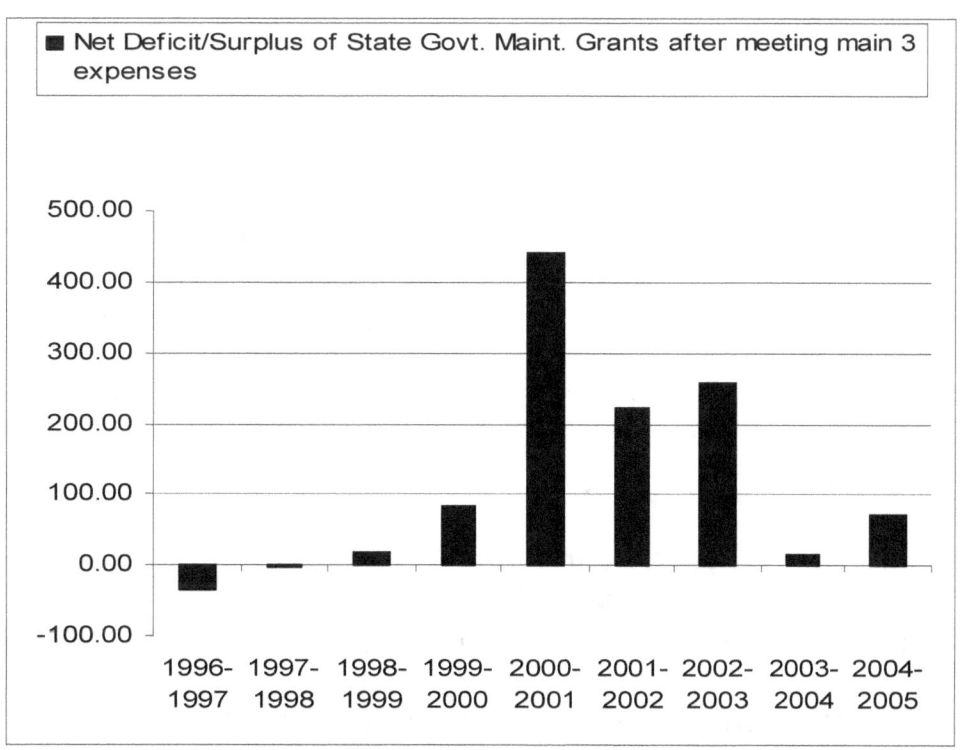

9. Health Centre Expenditure to Other Fees Income

Table 4.19 Health Centre Expenditure to Other Fees Income Ratio

Years	Health Centre	Other Fees	Ratio	Difference
1996-1997	4.97	12.87	38.59%	7.91
1997-1998	9.09	15.96	56.97%	6.87
1998-1999	7.50	20.48	36.61%	12.98
1999-2000	9.67	47.64	20.31%	37.97
2000-2001	7.45	-3.63	205.44%	-11.07
2001-2002	11.09	64.17	17.28%	53.08
2002-2003	15.67	66.94	23.41%	51.27
2003-2004	13.53	76.12	17.77%	62.60
2004-2005	15.87	77.51	20.48%	61.64

From table 4.19 it is seen that the ratio remains very less throughout the research period else in the year 2000-01 when other fees income is negative and the health centre expenditure is 7.45lakhs but it is recovered from the heads like state government grant or examination expenditure which are having surplus in itself in that particular year. Here the ratio rotates in between 17.28% to 56.97% else in the year when it is negative it climbs highest by 205.44%. The ratio is 38.59% in 1996-97, after that it is more by 56.97% but this is not because health centre expenditure is high in this year but because proportionately of increasing in expenditure other fees has not increased in that year. After this in the year 1999-00 the expenditure reduces to 7.50lakhs and other fees income increases to 20.48% due to which again the ratio reduces to 36.61%. Than in the year 2000-01 the ratio is high by 205.44%. In the year 2001-02 the ratio reduces to 17.28% this is because the other fees income that was -3.63lakhs in 2001 has climbed to 64.17lakhs this is a huge climb again the expenditure has also increased to 11.09lakhs but not in this proportion so the ratio has reduced from 205.44% to 17.28%. After that the ratio rotates in between 17.77% to 23.41%. The other fees income from 12.87lakhs climbs to 77.51lakhs due to which again the university surplus increases, again the load of the minute sharing expenditure get reduces from the heads of state government grant and examination fees head. In table 4.19 it is clearly seen that after meeting health centre expenditure it is having surplus and that also in handsome lakhs.

10. Net Surplus or Deficit transferred to General Fund A/C including exam fees and excluding exam fees

Table 4.20 Net Surplus or Deficit transferred to General Fund A/C

including exam fees and excluding exam fees

(Amount in Lakhs)

Year	Surplus/Deficit transferred to General Fund A/C including exam fees	Surplus/Deficit transferred to General Fund A/C excluding exam fees net	Difference (net surplus of examination fees)
1996-1997	-29.48	-21.41	-8.06
1997-1998	18.00	-8.75	-9.25
1998-1999	4.29	-37.83	33.53
1999-2000	166.55	77.05	89.50
2000-2001	360.20	239.56	120.65
2001-2002	320.74	205.22	115.53
2002-2003	341.22	222.17	119.06
2003-2004	210.87	55.86	155.01
2004-2005	250.88	126.68	124.20

Note:-

The surplus or deficit that researcher has found in financial statements are deficit or surplus excluding exam fees. The Saurashtra university has followed the format that can be said as mixed format

which means that in the years 1996-97 and 1997-98 they have included them in Revenue Income and Expenditure A/c, and after that from 1998-99 to 2004-05 they have shown them separately in individual examination account. As per the accounting principle this is revenue income so the researcher has treated the same as revenue and shown the same jointly in revenue income and expenditure account so that it can reveal the true financial position of the business.

From the table 4.20 given above we can see that the net surplus or deficit of general fund account including exam fees is in deficit only in the year that is 1996-97 by -29.48lakhs. In this particular year exam fee net is also in deficit as it shows that the deficit excluding exam fee in 1996-97 is -21.41lakhs. The loss excluding exam fee is less by -8.06lakhs which is the net deficit of examination account.

After that in all other years of research period revenue income and expenditure account including exam fees has done profit. The exam fees also have the net surplus in the remaining research period. The profit is at highest point in the year 2000-2001 by 360.20lakhs and the reason for the same were in this particular year State Government Maintenance Grant received is maximum and as compared to the same the main expenditure like Salary Expenditure and Advertisement Expenditure are minimum in this year.

In 1997-98 the profit is by 18lakhs this is comparatively low profit comparing to the other years. The profit has to bear the heavy loss of post graduate department which is -21.17lakhs which is a heavy loss comparing to other years and the estate section has also born a loss of -15.43lakhs which is huge amount comparing to its proportion of rise in income. Again the state government maintenance grant in this year has shown just a rise by 105.53lakhs as compared to last year and as we have seen that is occupied only to meet the main 3 expenditures of university and in that also it is bearing the loss of -2.18lakhs again many other expenditure are yet to be deducted like adhoc bonus of 8.94lakhs and encashment of leave expenditure of

9.73lakhs, physical education of 3.30lakhs,etc. The income from other heads remains limited in this period and their share does not show a huge rise comparatively to other research period. The maintenance of building expenditure is allotted in this year by 7.30lakhs. The administrative expenditure and Salary expenditure has shown rise in this year by 18.87lakhs and 39.22lakhs, yet the hostel and library loss is not calculated as the loss are negligible due to all this reason the profit in this year is limited comparing to other years. In this year if we consider examination surplus than we have profit as the surplus is 26.75lakhs if we do not consider the same as revenue surplus the university bears a loss of -8.75lakhs.

In 1998-99 the net surplus is lowest by -4.29lakhs including exam fees and if we exclude exam fees the than it has loss by -37.83lakhs. In this year the rise in grant received from State government for maintenance is by 160.98lakhs as compared to last year. Compared to last year the salary expenditure has shown a huge rise by 148.64lakhs. In this year Vth pay commission arrears of 39.08lakhs are paid which are not paid in the past period.

The encashment of leave expenditure is increased by 3.66lakhs. The deficit of post graduate department, library, hostel, estate that was there in the last year is continued in this year also. All the deficits are having minor changes. They have continued as the same only. Again all the expenses have increased in equal proportion. So because of all these reasons there is again a highest deficit of -37.83lakhs in this year excluding exam fees or a lowest surplus by 4.29lakhs including exam fees.

In 1999-00 including exam fee there is a profit of 166.55lakhs and excluding exam fees profit of 77.05lakhs. In this year comparing to last year the state government maintenance grant increased by 205.64lakhs. This is a huge increase. In this year the library net deficit and estate net deficit has increased by -7.74lakhs and -17.05lakhs. In this year other fees income has increased by 27.16lakhs. Post graduate department net deficit has reduced by 3.68lakhs. Salary expenditure has increased by 118.98lakhs. This year expenditure of capital nature has been added which was charged by 8.47lakhs. This year state government grant is enough to carry the three main expenses and has a surplus net by 82.56lakhs. This year state government grant has shown huge rise and again expenditure are increased but not in proportion to it and income have also shown minor rise. Due to all this they have profit by 77.05lakhs excluding exam fees and 166.55lakhs including exam fees.

In 2000-01 the net surplus including exam fees is 360.20lakhs and excluding exam fees is 239.56lakhs. The net surplus is highest in this year and this is the year in which we received the highest state government grant by 1275.66lakhs and rise comparing to last year by 359.01lakhs. In this year comparing to the last year Post graduate net deficit increases by 16.00lakhs. All the other deficit of library, estate and hostel shows the similar deficit or near by deficit as per the last year. The other fees income in this year got reduced by -51.27lakhs comparing to last year. The salary expenditure and the administrative expenditure that are the main expenditure of university got reduced in this year by -2.09lakhs and -8.86lakhs. The vth pay commission expenditure got increased in this year by 154.18lakhs. As comparing to the grant received all this expenditure or losses are very minute in this year else vth pay commission but the same is covered by the huge rise in grant.

In 2001-02 the net surplus including exam fees is 320.74lakhs and excluding exam fees is **205.22**lakhs. This year state government grant comparing to last year got reduced by -200.96lakhs. But as in this year the earthquake was there and the grant was maximum we will not consider the same as a last year and we will analyze 2001-02 with the year 1999-00 as base year. State government grant comparing to the year 1999-2000 yet shows increase by 158.05lakhs and in 1999-2000 also we have a surplus of 166.05 including exam fees and 77.05 excluding exam fees. The Post graduate department net deficit got increased by 0.91lakhs. The estate deficit got increased by 26.78lakhs. The library net deficit got reduced by 5.48lakhs. The deficit of hostel shows the similar deficit or near by deficit as per the last year. The other fees income in this year gets a huge rise by 67.79lakhs comparing to last year. This is a strategic turn for this year. The salary expenditure got reduced in this year by -1.91lakhs and administrative expenditure shows a rise by 3.55lakhs. Encashment of leave expenditure got rise in this year by 8.17lakhs. The vth pay commission expenditure got increased in this year by 36.59lakhs. Although the expenditure has increased but as compare to the year 1999-00 this increase is not touching the surplus because the grant received is more by 1999-00 by 166.06lakhs again other fees shows rise by 67.79lakhs. The total surplus of both of them is 233.85lakhs again add the net surplus of 1999-00 which is also 77.05 excluding exam fees so net surplus becomes 310.90lakhs. With this total surplus the deficit or rise in expenditure is very minute. Thus the surplus is achieved like this strategy in this year by increasing grant and other fees income and expenditure not showing proportion rise.

In 2002-03 including exam fee there is a profit of 341.22lakhs and excluding exam fees profit of 222.17lakhs. In this year comparing to last year the state government maintenance grant reduced by 158.65lakhs.

The post graduate deficit got increased by 18.07lakhs compared to last year 2002-03. In this year the library net deficit increased 3.46lakhs and estate net deficit decreased by -12.76lakhs. In this year other fees income has increased by 2.77lakhs and miscellaneous income increased by 8.46lakhs. The Salary and administrative expenditure has increased by 44.37lakhs and 18.43lakhs. This year the physical education expenditure got increased by 37.73lakhs. The vth pay commission got reduced by 20lakhs. The net surplus of last year 250.22lakhs excluding exam fees and rise in state government grant by 99.10lakhs and total of the same by 349.32 is a huge amount to meet all the expenses rise and deficits.

In 2003-04 including exam fee there is a profit of 210.87lakhs and excluding exam fees profit of 55.86lakhs. In this year comparing to last year the state government maintenance grant decreased by 158.65lakhs. The post graduate deficit got increased by 10.59lakhs compared to last year 2001-02. In this year the library net deficit increased by -2.93lakhs and estate net deficit has decreased by 4.71lakhs. In this year other fees income has increased by 9.19lakhs. The Salary expenditure has increased by 67.65lakhs and administrative expenditure has decreased by -1.96lakhs. This year the physical education expenditure decreased by -34.41lakhs. The encashment of leave expenditure got decreased by 5.77lakhs. The vth pay commission got reduced by 10.62lakhs. The net surplus of last year 220.17lakhs excluding exam fees and decrease in state government grant by 158.65lakhs and total of the same by 61.52 is a small amount to meet all the expenses and again rise in salary expenditure by 67.65lakhs has reduced the profit to 55.86 excluding exam fees. This year the university was to move to deficit but due to rise by 9.19lakhs in other fees and cutoff in physical education expenditure, encashment leave expenditure, and vth pay commission, and minor increase and decrease in other expenditure has left it with surplus.

In 2004-05 including exam fee there is a profit of 250.88lakhs and excluding exam fees profit of 126.68lakhs. In this year comparing to last year the state government maintenance grant increased by 34.85lakhs. The post graduate deficit got increased by 12.20lakhs compared to last year 2001-02. In this year the library net deficit decreased by 6.86lakhs and estate net deficit has increased by 12.98lakhs. In this year other fees income has increased by 1.38lakhs and miscellaneous income by 5.97lakhs. The Salary expenditure has decreased by 30.04lakhs and administrative expenditure has decreased by 5.46lakhs. This year the physical education expenditure decreased by 3.71lakhs. The encashment of leave expenditure got decreased by 1.40lakhs. The vth pay commission got reduced by 1.03lakhs. The net surplus of last year 55.86lakhs excluding exam fees and increase in state government grant by 34.85lakhs and decrease in salary expenditure by 30.04lakhs and decrease in administrative expenditure by 5.46lakhs and total of the same by 126.21 is a rise in total income comparing to last year to meet the expenses, again the minor fluctuations in other income and expenditure has make it possible to earn the profit of 126.68lakhs excluding exam fees.

CHAPTER: 5
FINDINGS AND CONCLUSIONS
FINDINGS:-

1. As per table 4.14 after meeting all main 3 expenses state government maintenance grant has surplus in all the years of research period else in the year 1996-97 and 1997-98 this is because the basic grant received in this year was less than its total expenditure. In 1998-99 the grant received was increased by 105.53lakhs but than also it was not able to meet the main 3 heads of expenditure this years were in loss because basically the grant received during this year compare to their expenditure was very low.

2. The state government grant has played a main role for turnaround. The procurement of State government grant started increasing in the loss period and it was highest in 2000-01, this is the year in which the university has done maximum net surplus this is because of earthquake a heavy grant

was received. Normally the turnaround started from the year 1998-99 this is basic year when the grant was enough to meet all the revenue expenditure of university but after 2000-01 it starts declining but the declining was not up to the level of loss period. The declining was also able to give healthy net surplus to university.

3. As per the chart 4n you can see that after meeting all main expenditure state government maintenance grant have surplus in it in the years 1998 to 2005. The deficit is in the first two years that is 1996 and 1997. The surplus is maximum in 2000- 2001 by 401.12lakhs. From here it is seen that main turnaround period is from 1999-00 to 2002-03 after that again the surplus is there but comparatively it has started declining. And the deficit is in 1996-97 which has started reducing in 1997-98 and after that deficit getting transferred into surplus.

4. The other fees income also plays a healthy role in turnaround. The other fees income has risen from

12.87lakhs to 77.51lakhs. Every year the other fees grow is added to net surplus or is used to help the company to meet expenditure. The other fees income starts rising faster from 1999-00 than else in 2000-01 it continues to rise for the rest of the research period.

5. Salary Expenditure of university employees has shown a huge reduction from 61.93% to 49.76% in total revenue expenditure means a total decrease by 12.17% as compared to 1996-97. It shows a decreasing trend. No doubt the salary expenditure on record by amount has increased but not in proportion of increase in income from state government and other fees income. The salary expenditure has increased but in compare to it state government maintenance grant has increased at a high rate.

6. There is a very negligible change in university administrative expenditure in the accounting period means its share in total income has shows a minute

change from 1996-97 to 2004-05 comparing to rise in total income. Again administrative expenditure share in total expenditure has started reducing from 1998-99 and again after that it has never reached the highest point of 16.53% which was achieved in 1998-99. The university administrative expenditure in amount has increased but not in proportion with increase in grant or increase in other income or in some years it maintains a steady trend also in comparison.

7. The variations in exam fees income are negligible it shows steady trend as compare to the total income.

8. The examination expenditure plays a vital role for TURN AROUND. The changes in the Examination expenditure and income are not in equal proportion. Income in all the years of research period has surplus comparing to expenditure. The net surplus in examination income has increased by 784.76lakhs within research period. This is a huge amount for turnover.

9. The post graduate department has not shown any positive contribution in turnaround strategy. Again it has become a part of profit reduction every year. It expenditure remains high than its income throughout the research period. The rotation level of expenditure is also very high. Again the relation between income and expenditure of post graduate is also not equal in the research period. That means that the changes in them during the years are not in proportion of income and expenditure.

10. The estate income has increased in the research period but not in proportion with the heavy increase in estate expenditure. University has done huge expenditure for estate maintenance as compared to its income. The share of estate income and expenditure are minor but if we compare them estate section plays a vital role in cutting off the profit year to year. Again the Estate section loss rotates in between the amount of 15.43 lakhs to 59.12 lakhs. The loss remain less in the period

1996-99 and near by 15 to 16 lakhs but after they procured huge grant from state government in 2000-2001 the loss started increasing reached up to 59.12 lakhs. **But Estate section maintenance or development is basic requirement for university and expenditure on it is demanded time to time and it is necessary to provide the same.**

11. Hostel expense has increased from 1996-00 but than it has reduced a lot from 2001-05. It has reduced totally by 97% comparing to total income but its share is very minor. The net hostel has always shown a deficit in the research period else in the years 2002, 2003 and 2005. The hostel has started earning handsome income comparing to past years in 2004-05.

12. Library expense has also shown a net deficit in the research period. This shows it has no contribution in financial turnaround it has been apart of profit reduction but the library is source which in

itself should be enriched and so only university has done more expense in it comparing to its income. Library is the basic requirement of students and teachers of university and university has seen interest of them rather than net deficit.

13.   The Revenue Expenditure that has covered the minute or negligible share has shown very minute fluctuations. This type of expenditure is 0.00% for few years also. When we see them under individual head it shows minute share but when we combine them together that covers 1.00% to 1.50% share of total expenditure.

14.   All the revenue expenditure that we analyzed in that no expenditure has shown heavy increasing trend else salary expenditure and vth pay commission arrears. But again the rise in state government grant and other fees income has saved from the net deficit due to them in that years. Again the expenditure that has increasing trend in the same the increase is very minute like pension, adhoc,

bonus, etc. Normally, the increase move is from 0.01% to 2.00% average.

15.   Few expenditure of capital nature have been written off in particular year so this results in loss for that year but in the next year they are not available for decreasing net surplus.

16.   The turnaround strategy has not been achieved by itself for the same there is a proper plan for all the expenses and all the main income and it is achieved - this is the visionary insight for applied financial mechanism which has strengthened the university financially. (Proper Strategy adopted to turnaround from loss to profit).

CONCLUSIONS:-

- The university led by strong willpower to add value through viability has no alternative but to concentrate on the finance of the university.

- The universities should also adopt proper strategy for their sound existence and development like any other business organizations.

- A proper plan should be made in procuring non plan grant from state government as it is the main source of university revenue income and again with it only university will meet all the expenses throughout the year.

- University should also have handsome surplus with them to stand financially sound in the market and to meet all the basic facilities to enrich their students.

- Student allocation partially up to some point is demanded to meet the present competitive education market.

- The time to re-conceptualize universities entity from nonprofit to surplus to serve.

- University should earn revenue to the extent required to provide good education to students but it should not be a profit making organization.

BIBLIOGRAPHY

(Books)

Azad J L	A critical Study of the financing of Higher Education in India
Azad J.L.	"Financing of Higher education in India"
	Sterling publishers, New Delhi 1975
Dr. Shah K.R. & Dr. Srikantiah S.	Education Earnings and Income Distribution
	Deep & Deep Publications New Delhi
Dr. Sharma S.N.	Financial Administration and Budgets
	RBSA Publishers, Jaipur
Dr. Chauhan P.L.	Financial Decision making strategy
	Saurashtra University, Rajkot
	F.D.P. year 200-01 I.I.M. Ahmedabad
Dr. Chauhan P.L.	Accounting for services - A case study S.U.
	Indian Journal of Accounting June 2000, page 55
Garg V.P.	Financing Higher education

Radha Publications, New Delhi

Heggade O.D.   Finances and cost of higher education in India

Mohi Publications, New Delhi

Kothari C.R.   Research Methodology methods & Techniques

Lakadawala
&
Shah K.R.   A research paper on "optimum utilization of educational expenditure in Gujarat & Financing of university in Gujarat" economic & political weekly 1975

Mridula   Educational statistics at a glance

Bibliography of Higher Education in India.

Mathur B. L.   Financial Management

RBSA Publishers, Jaipur

Mansukhani G.S.   Crises in Indian Universities studies in Indian education series -1

Nanjundappa D. M.   Finance and management of higher education.

Deep & Deep Publications, New Delhi

ARTICLES

Azad A L State Governments grant to colleges AIU, New Delhi, 1981

Dutt Ruder, Costing of Correspondence Education – Need for a rational Policy", AIU, New Delhi – 1981

Dr. Nigam M S Rajasthan University Finances – A Case study

Gerg V P Finances of the University of Punjab : A Trend Analysis", AIU New Delhi, 1981

Kamat A R Financial of Higher Education : A Socio political Analysis of the Basic issues Khosla Sudha &

Khosla Pratibha, University Finance : A Note on statistics limitations